A
is for
Abstract

ADELE KUVITTAJA

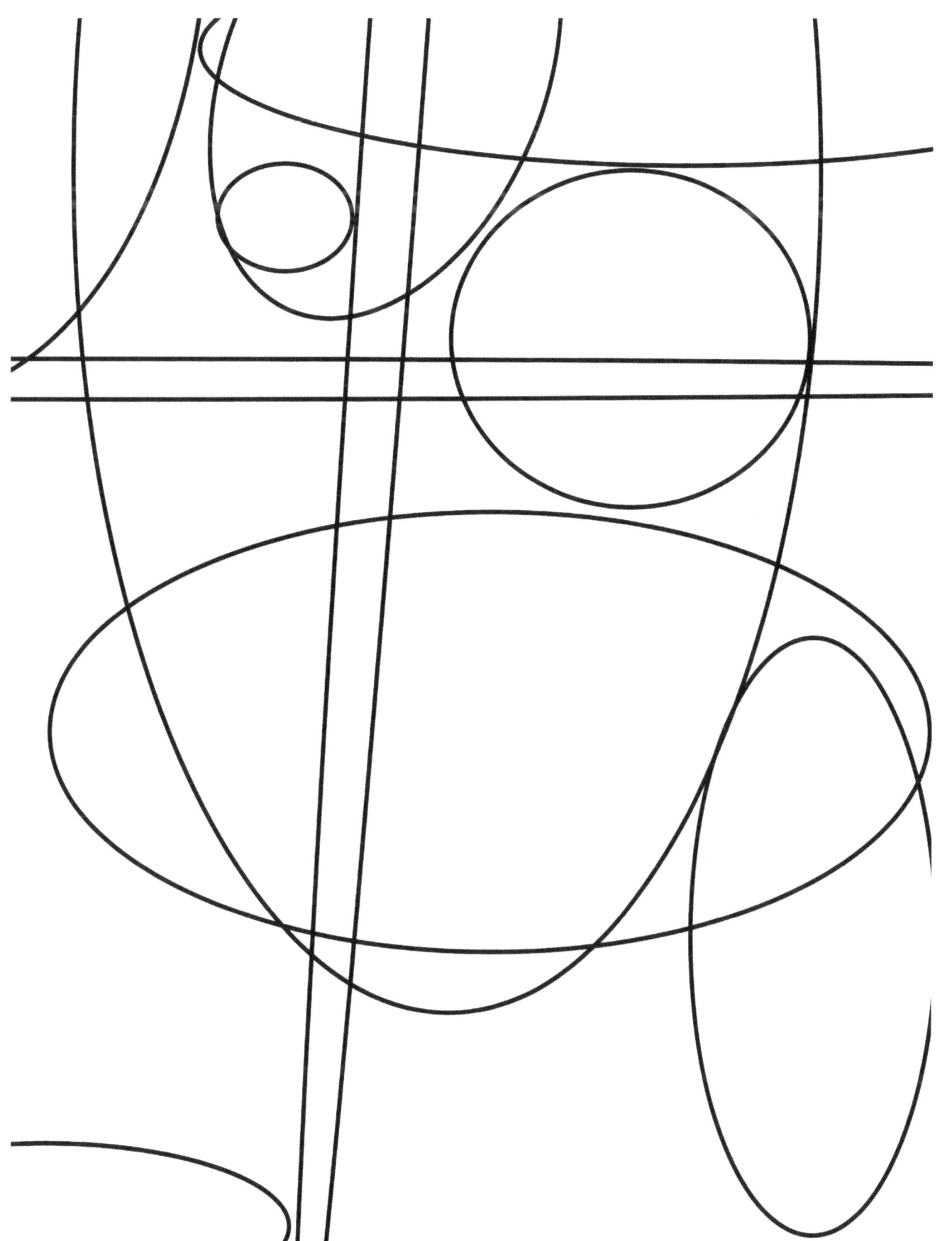

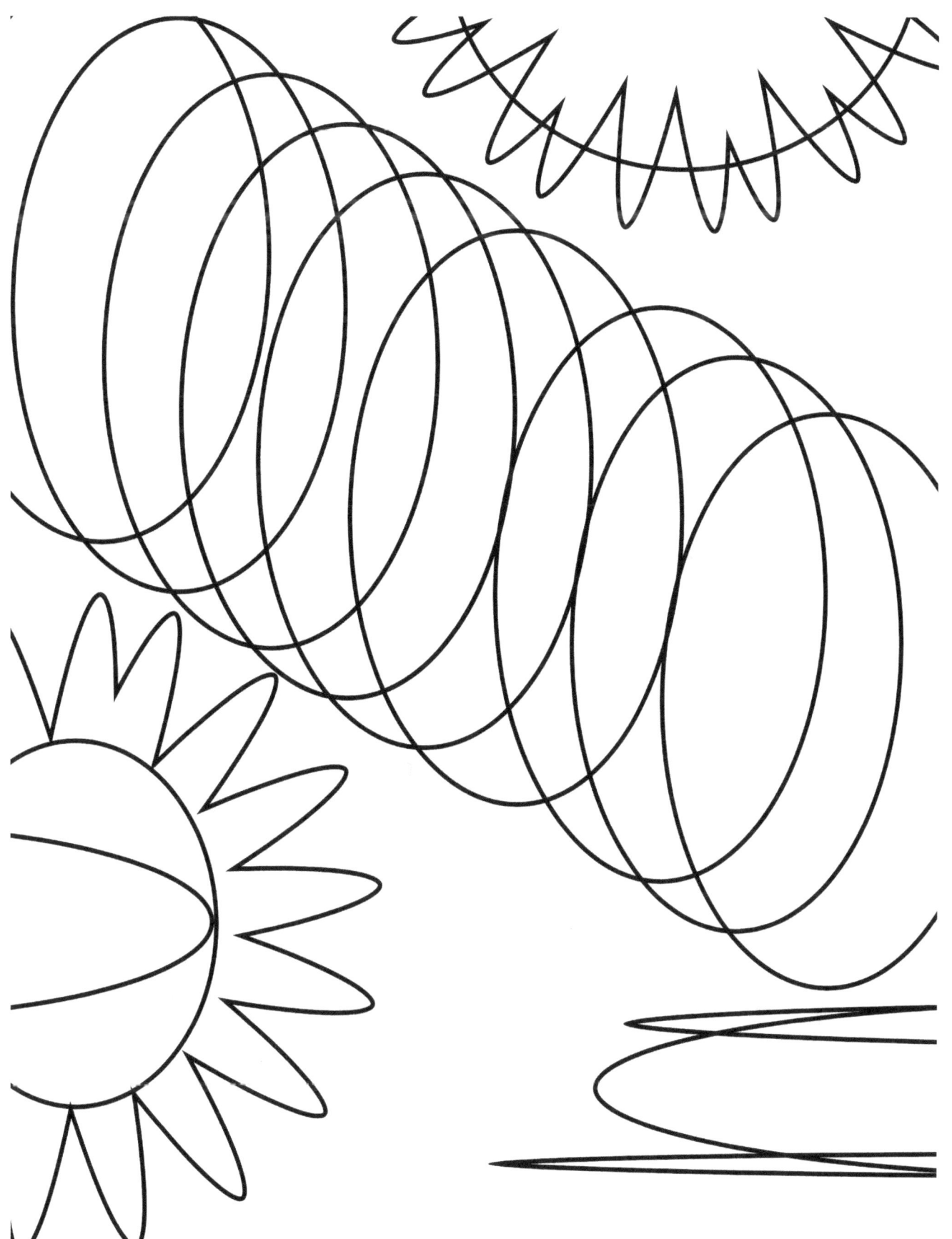

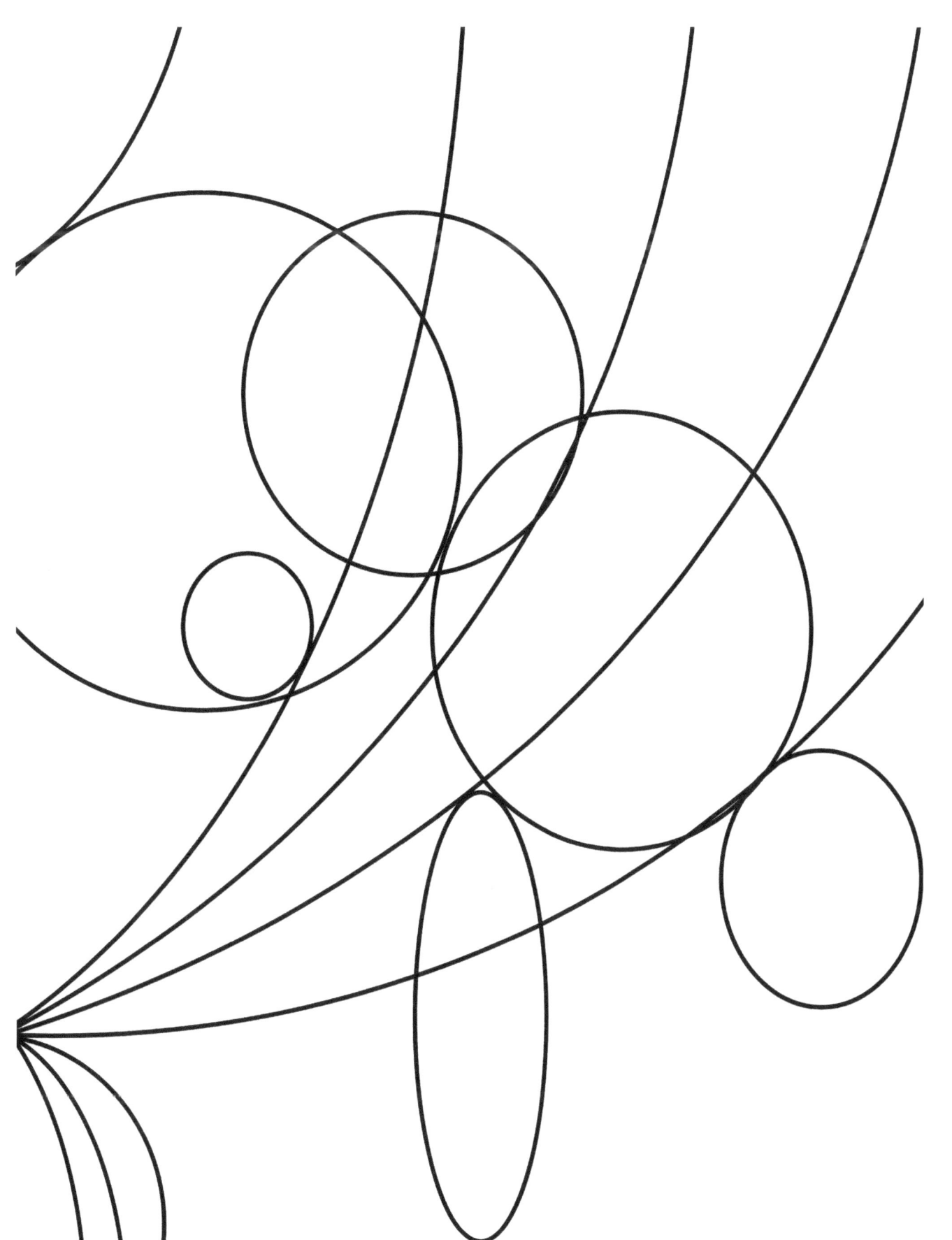

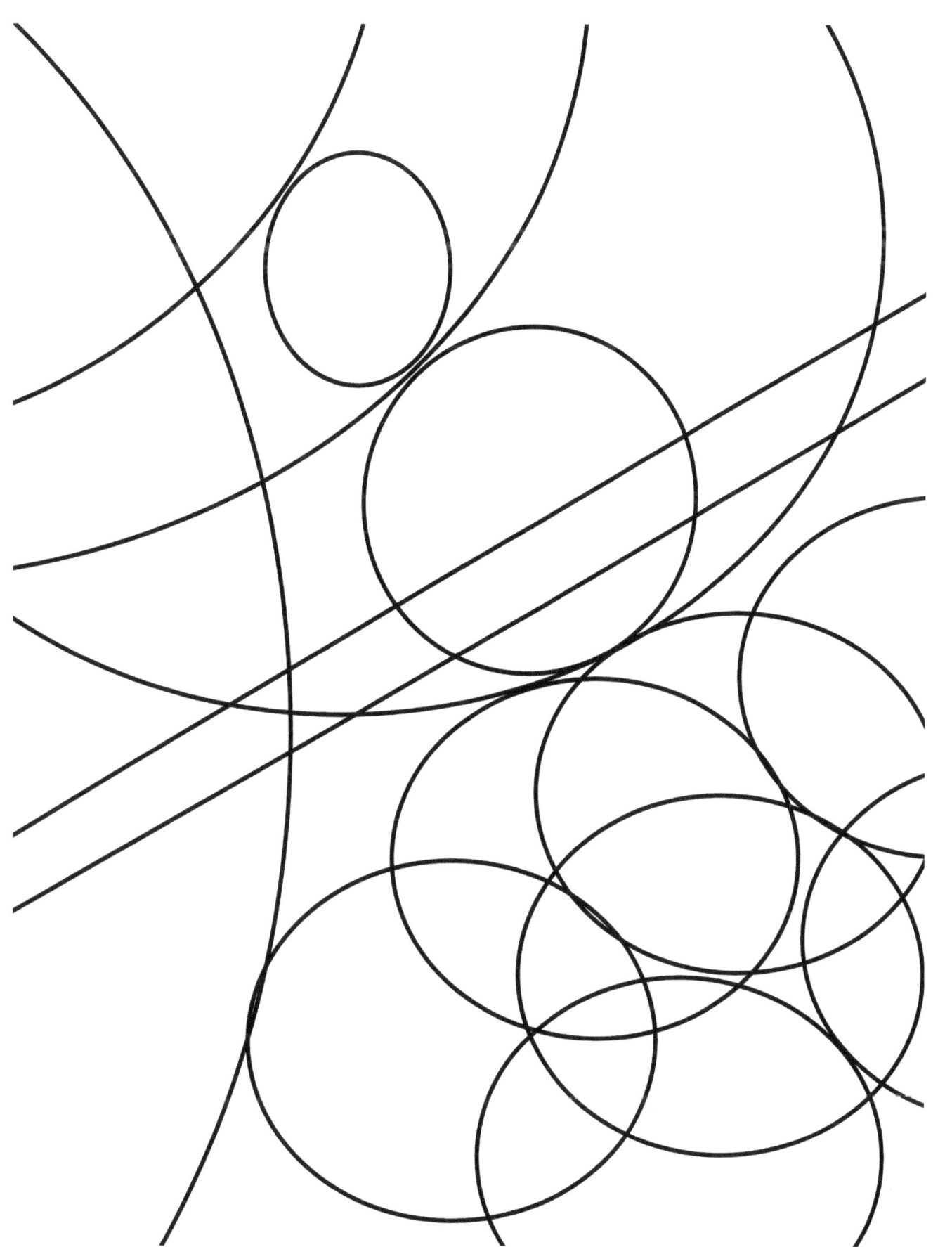

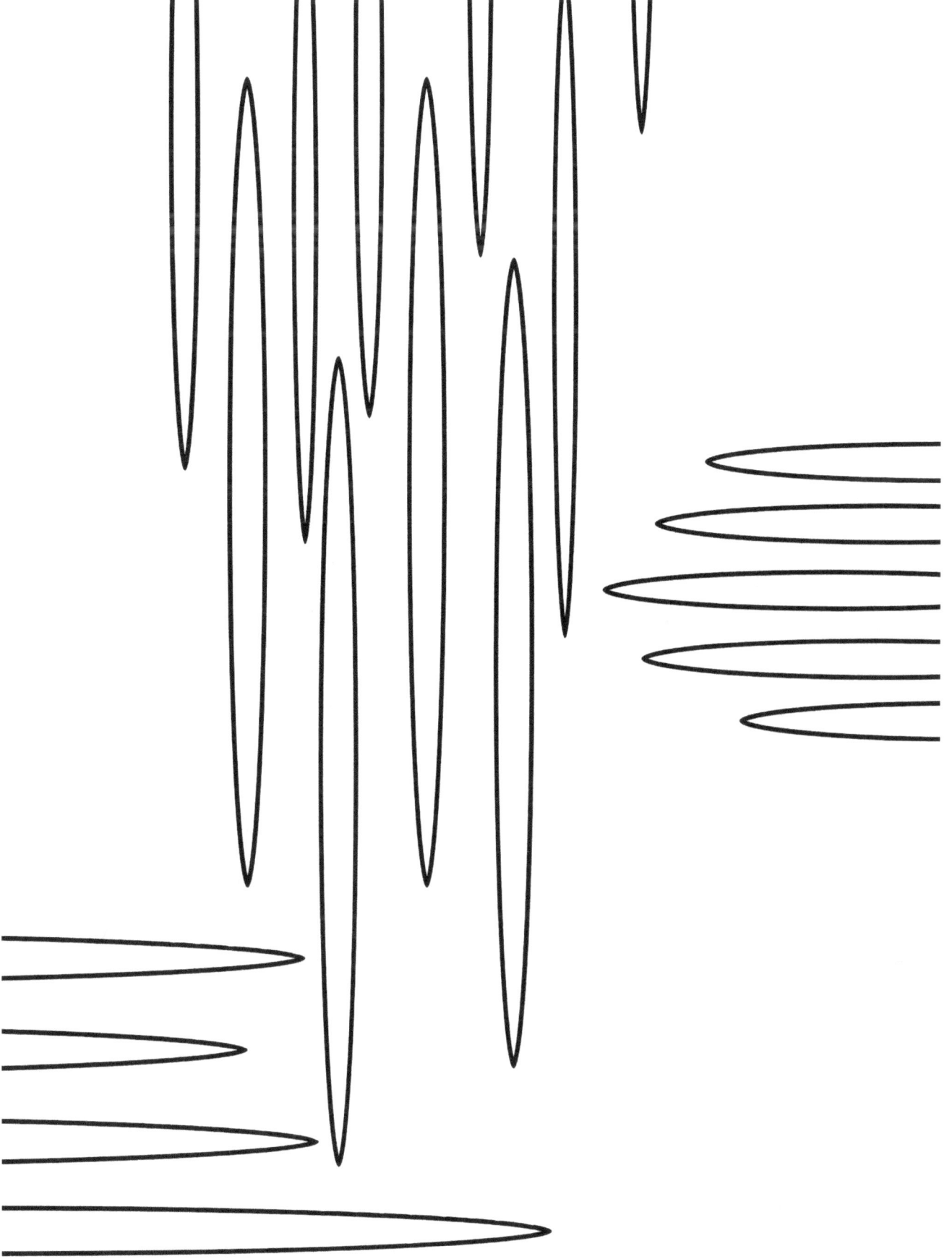

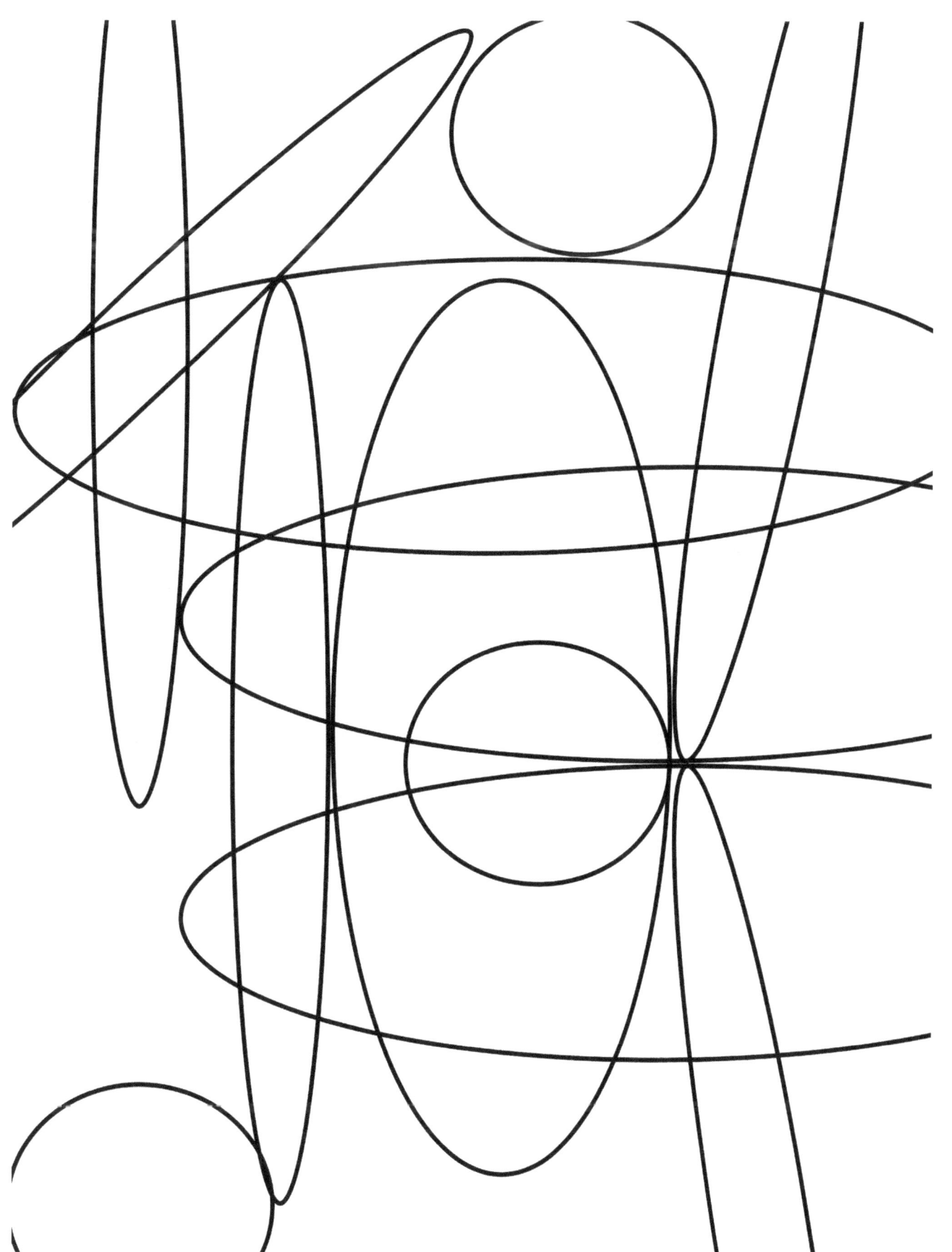

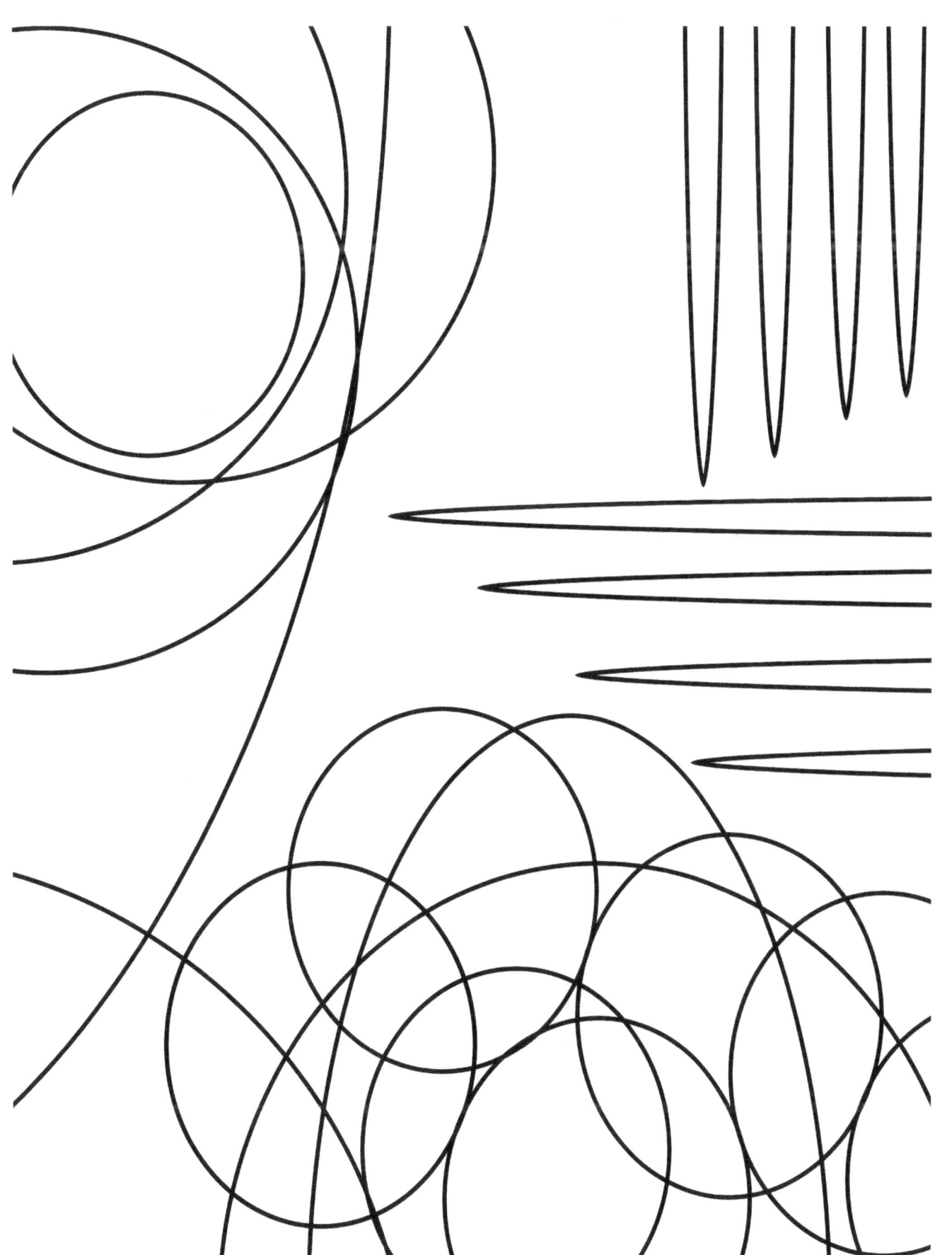

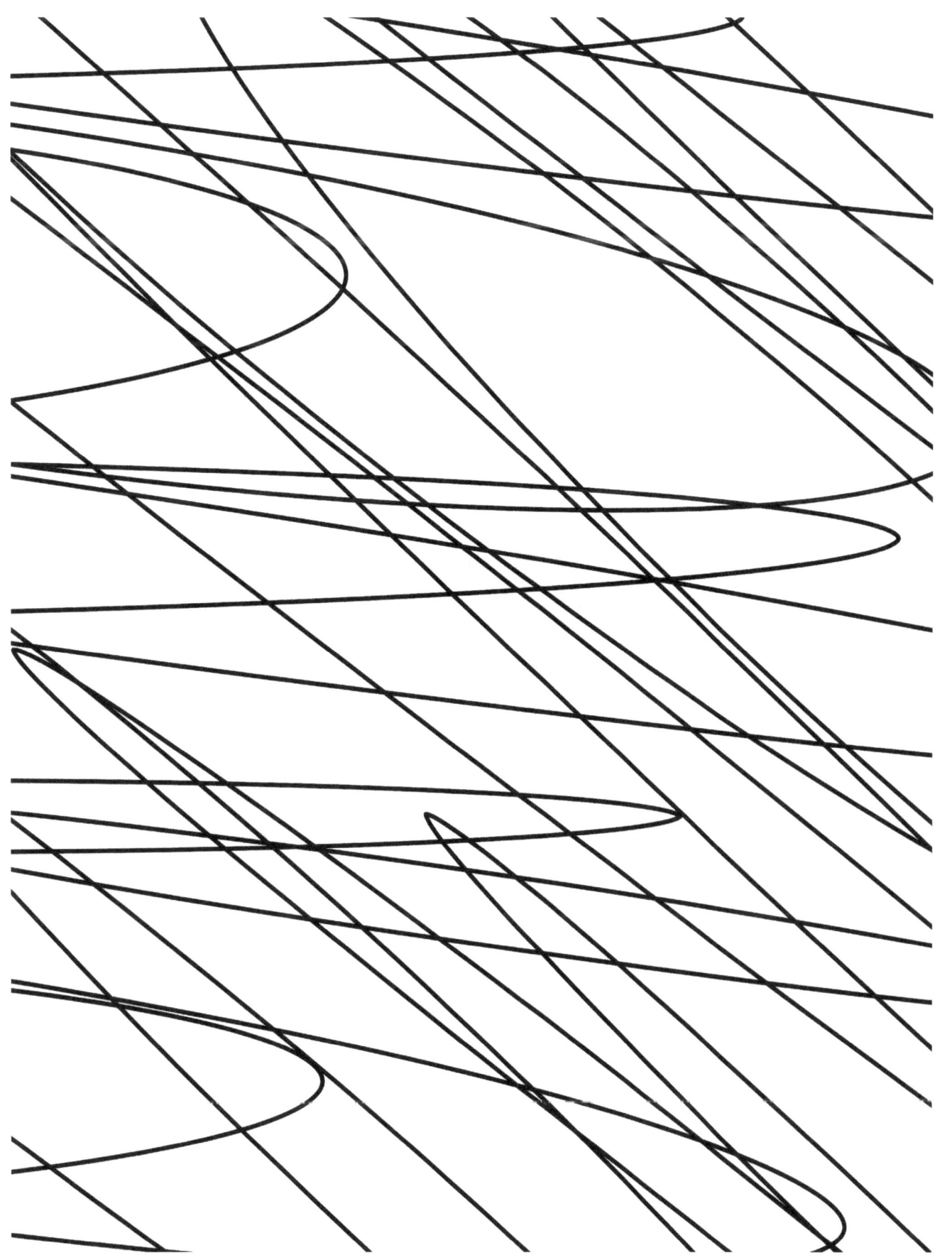

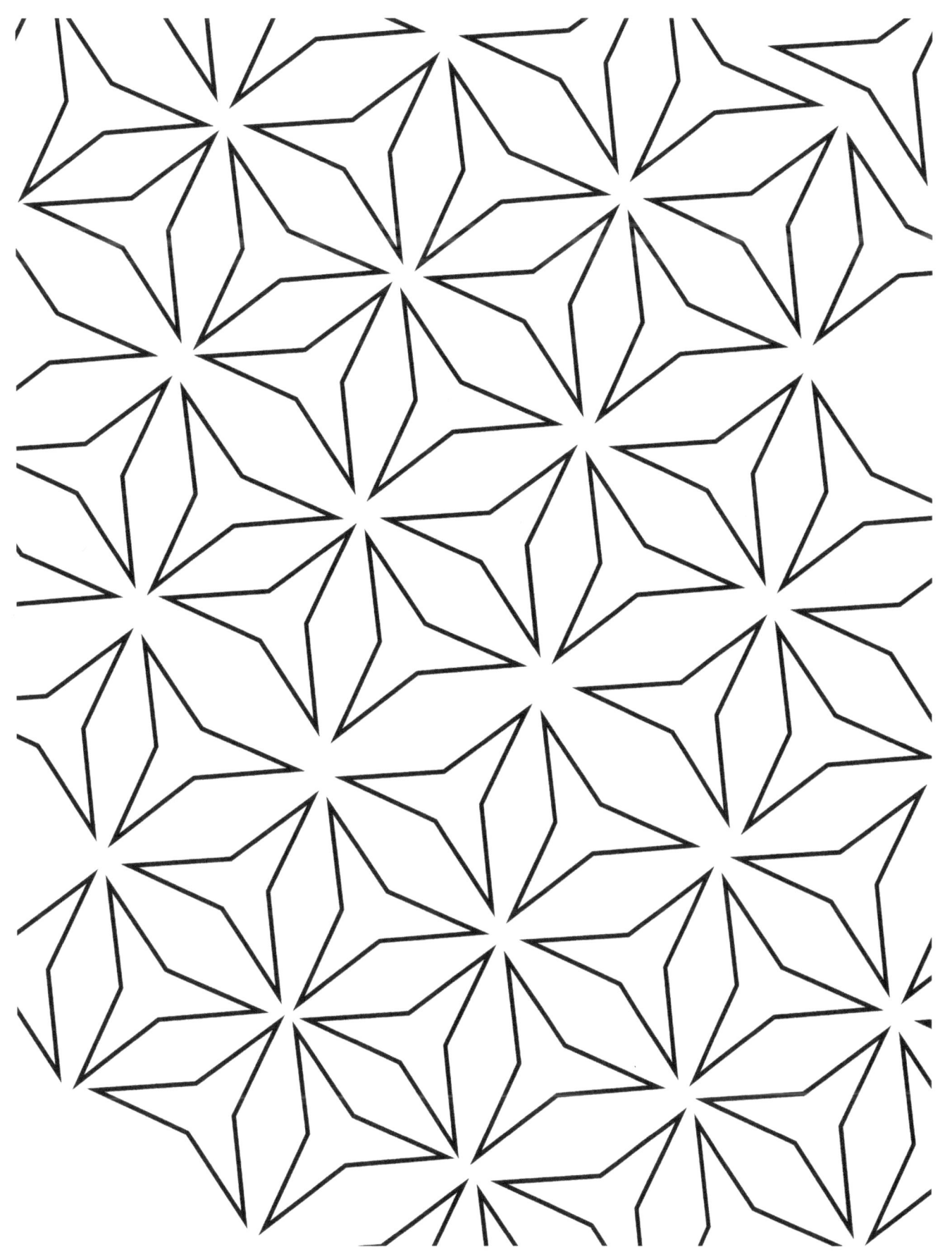

Abstract #9
Adele Kuvittaja

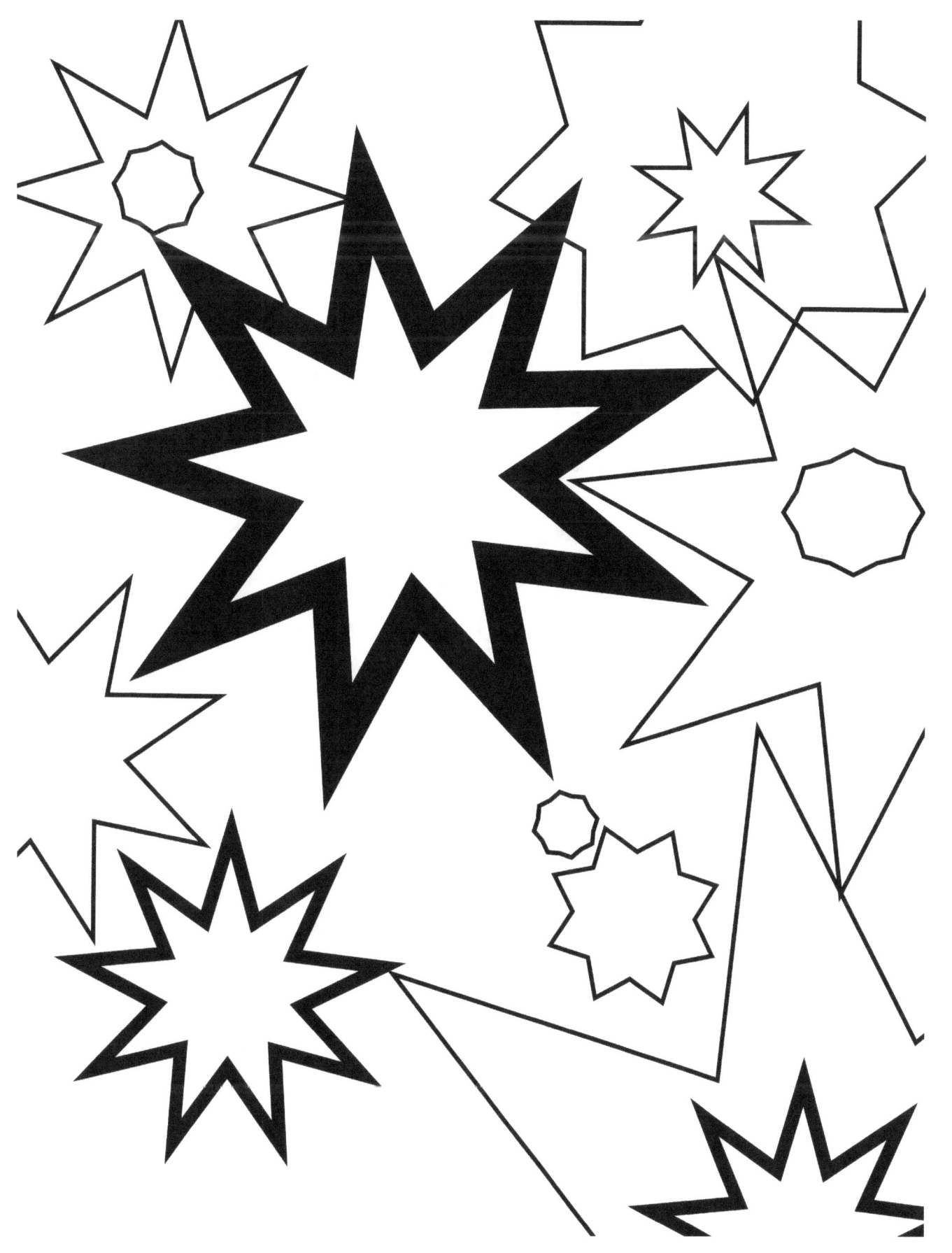

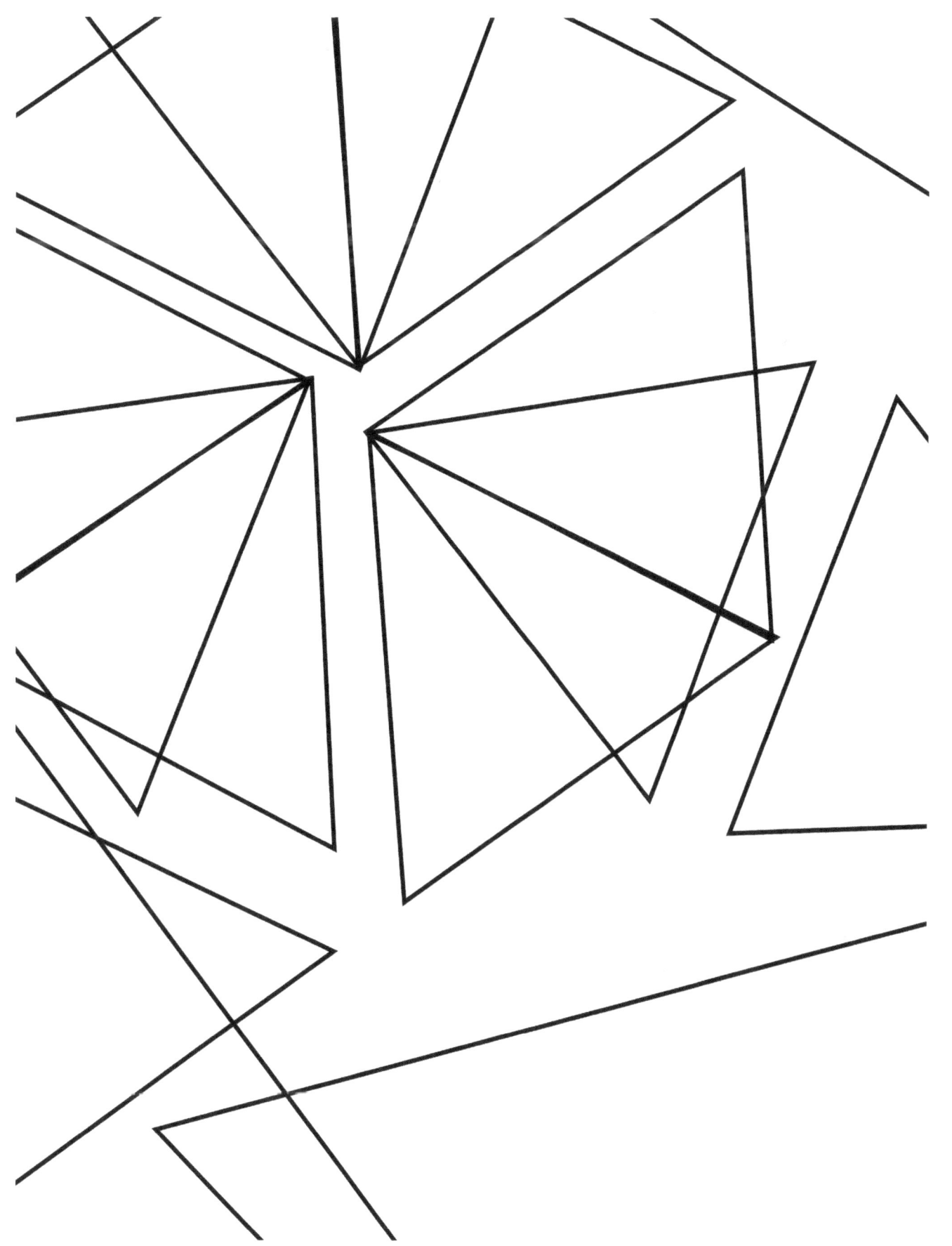

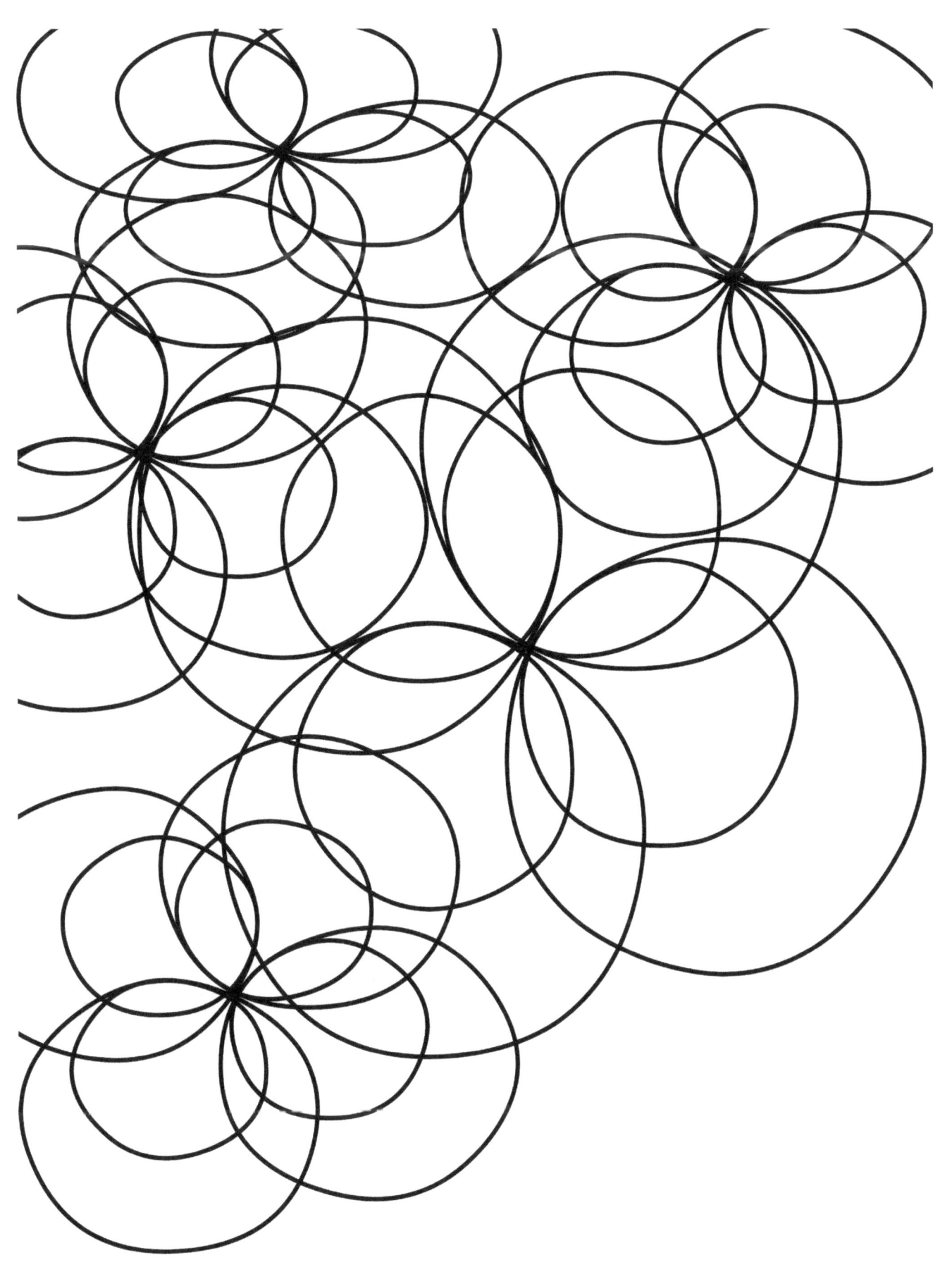

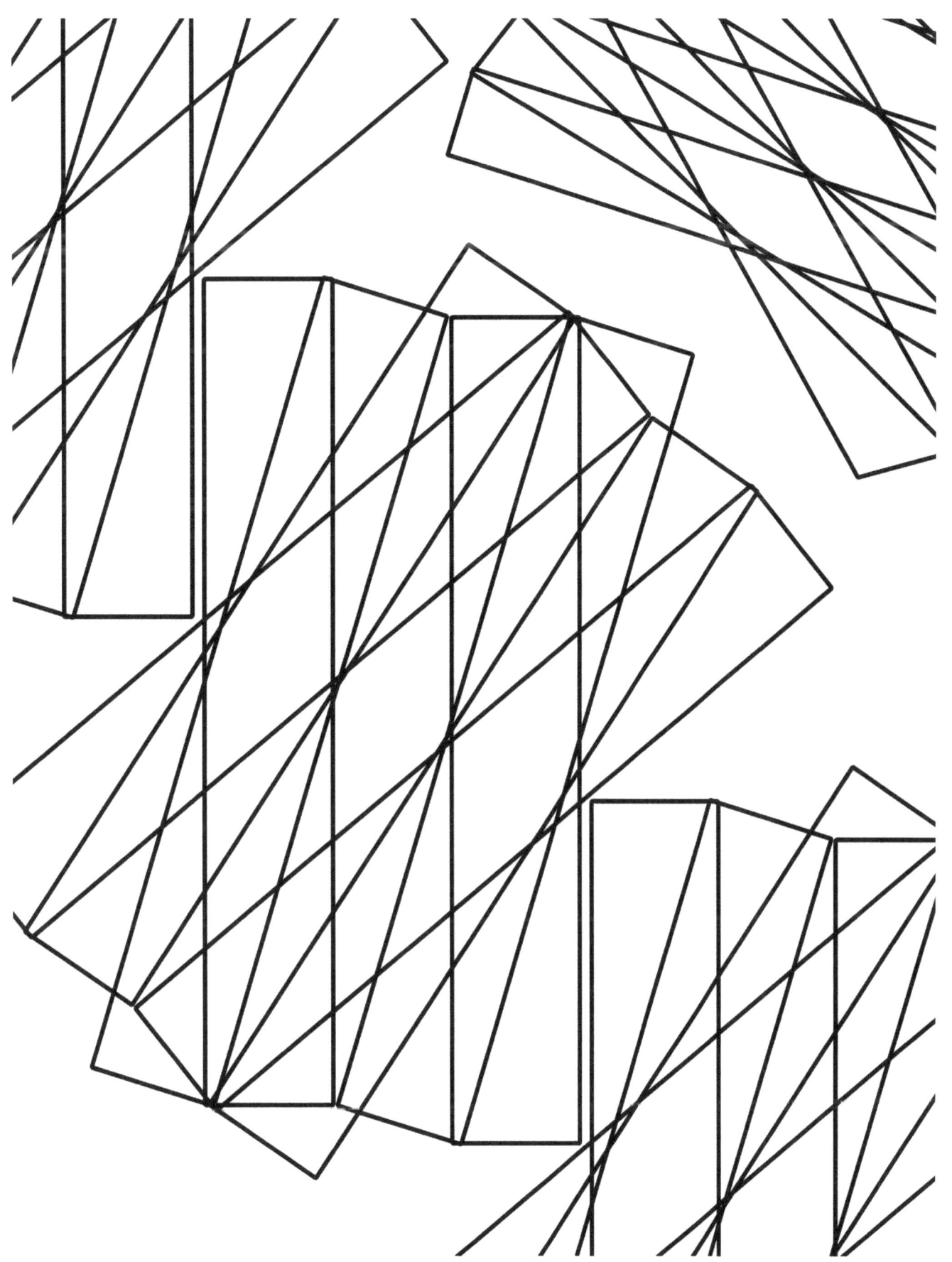

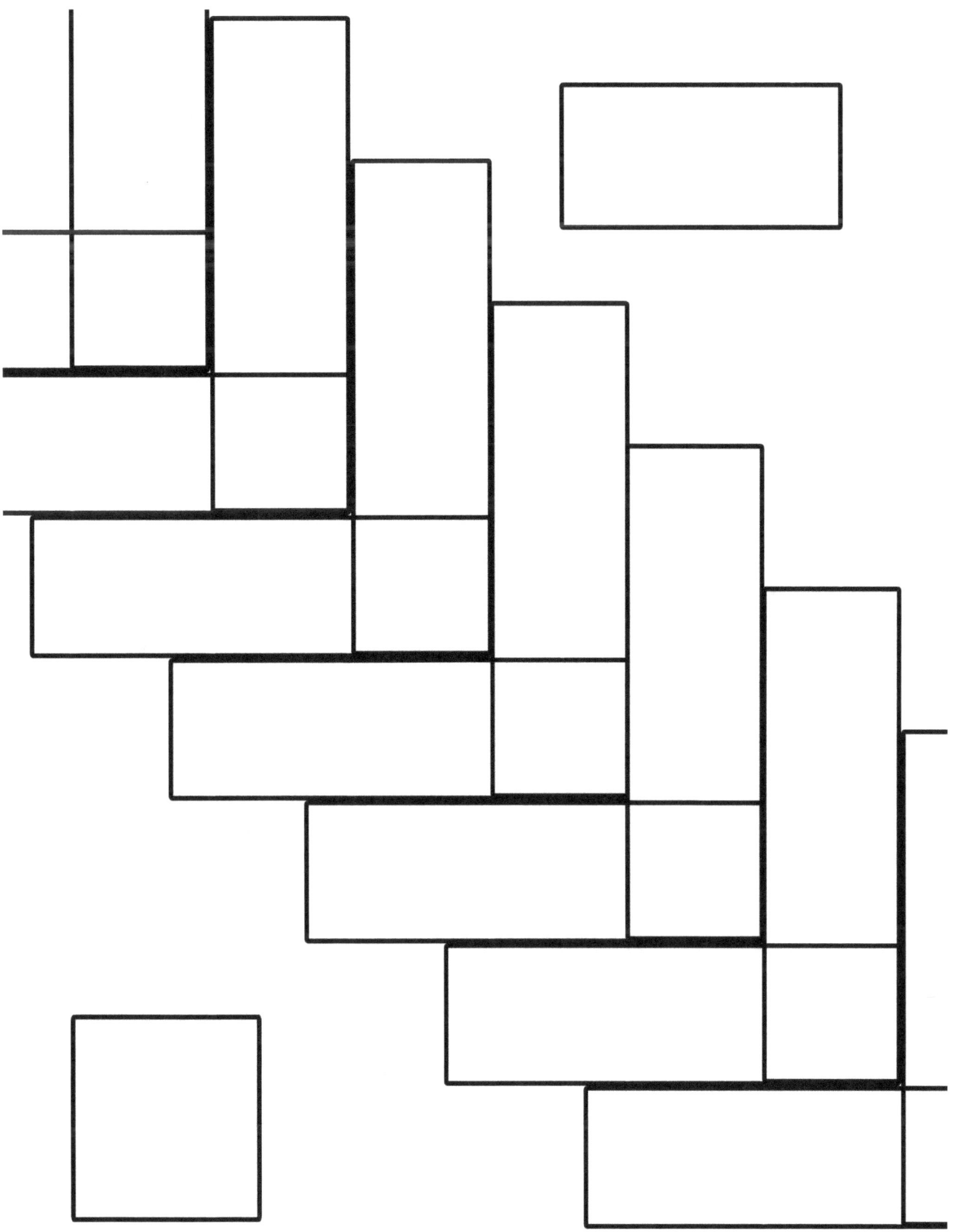

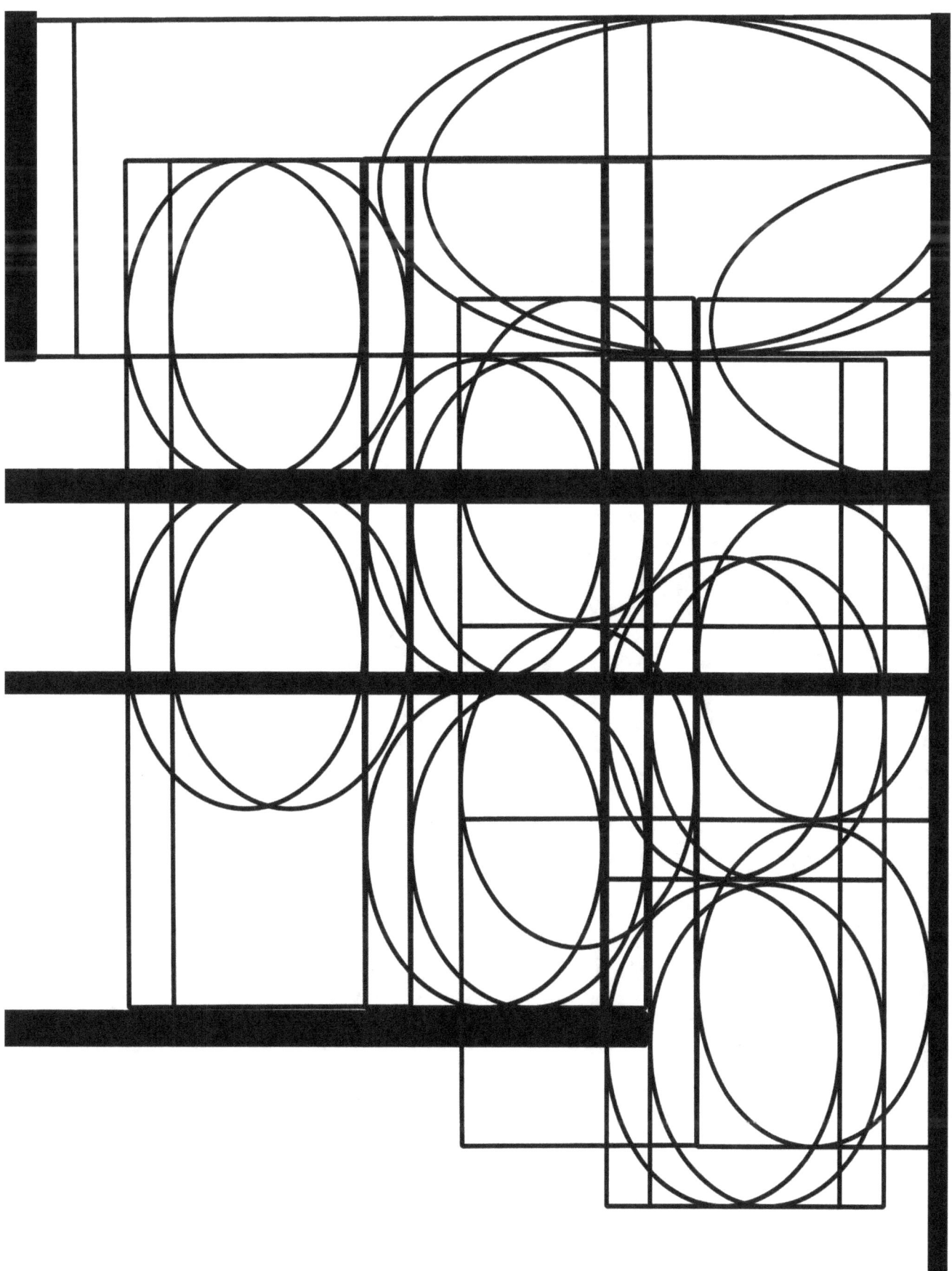

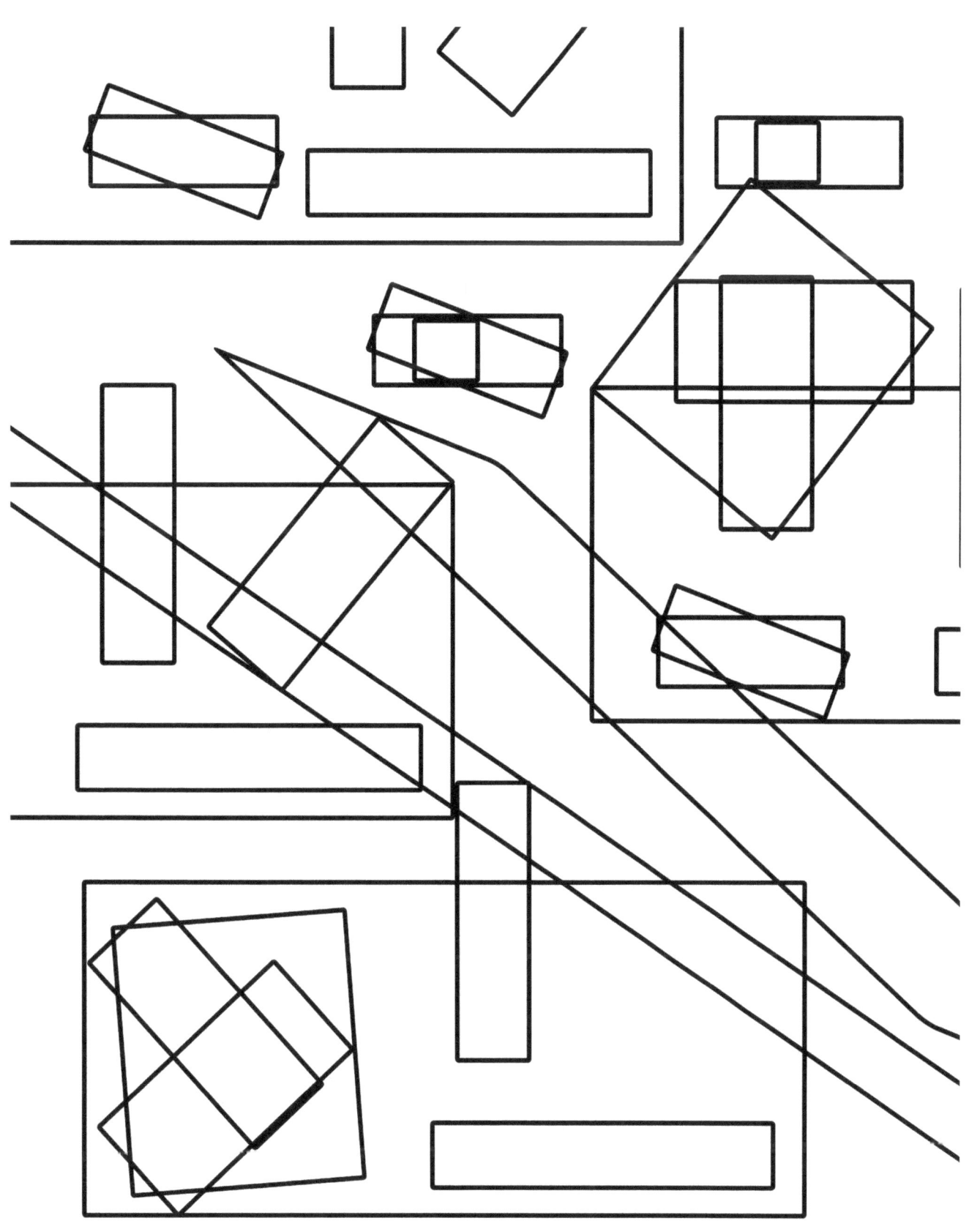

Abstract #16
Adele Kuvittaja

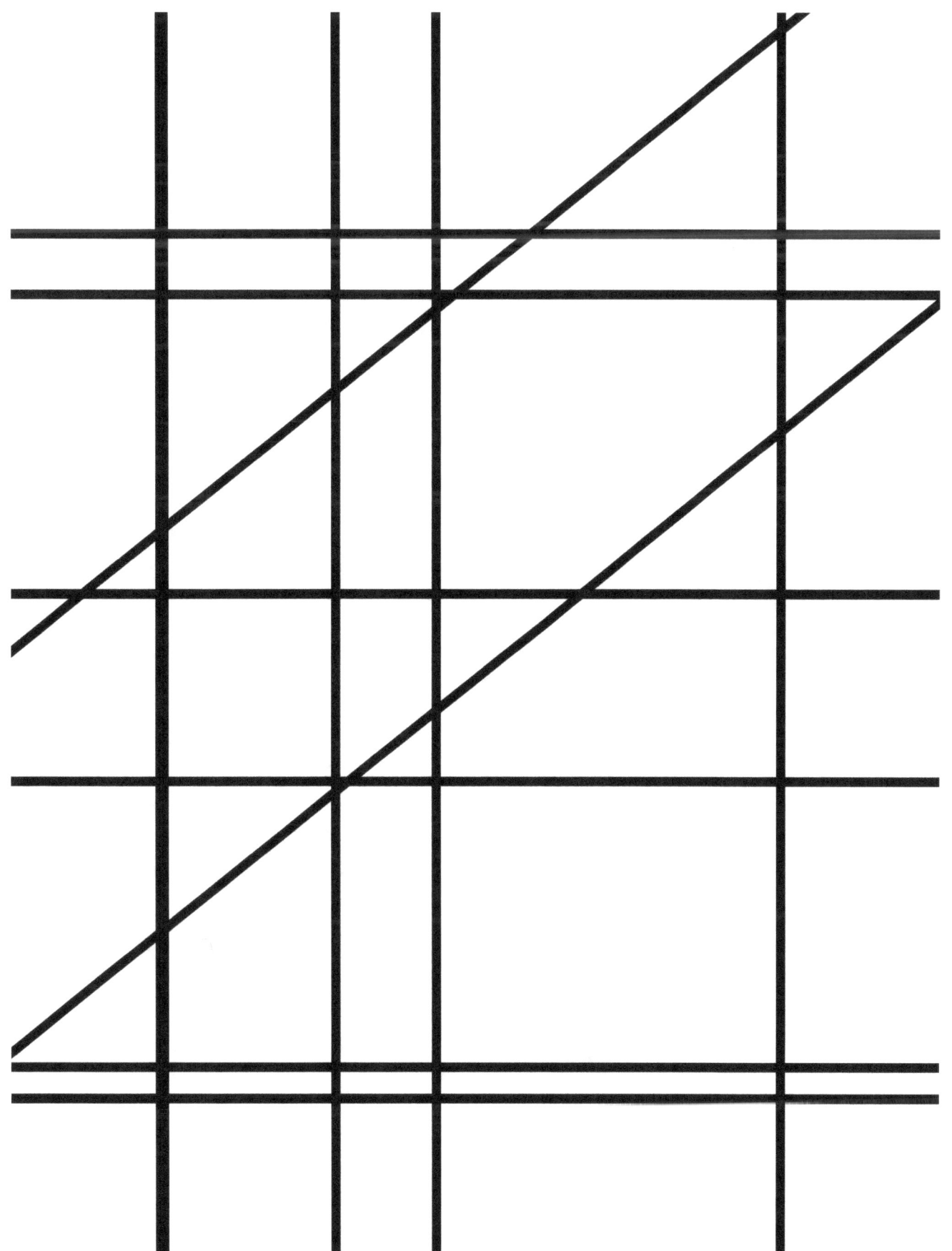

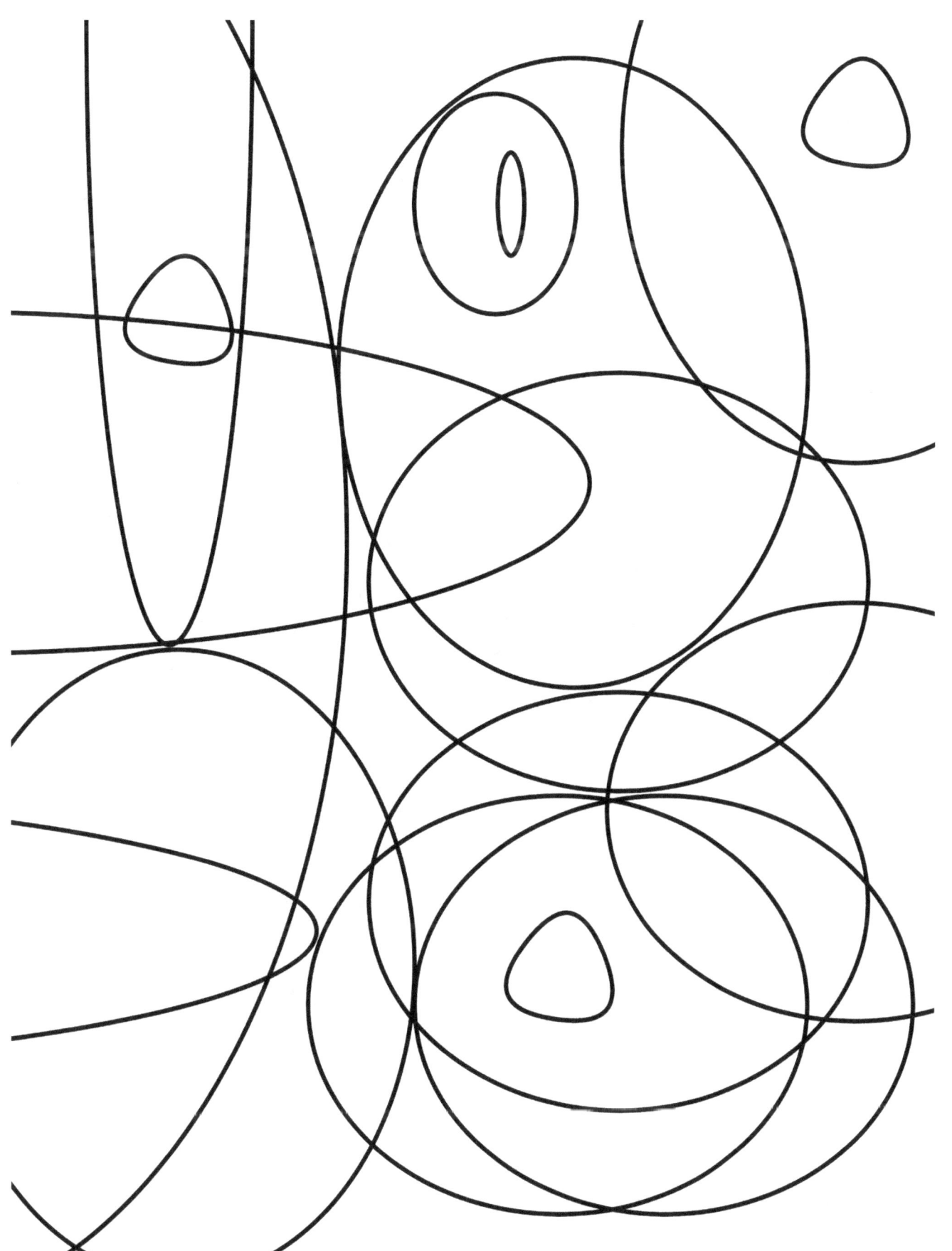

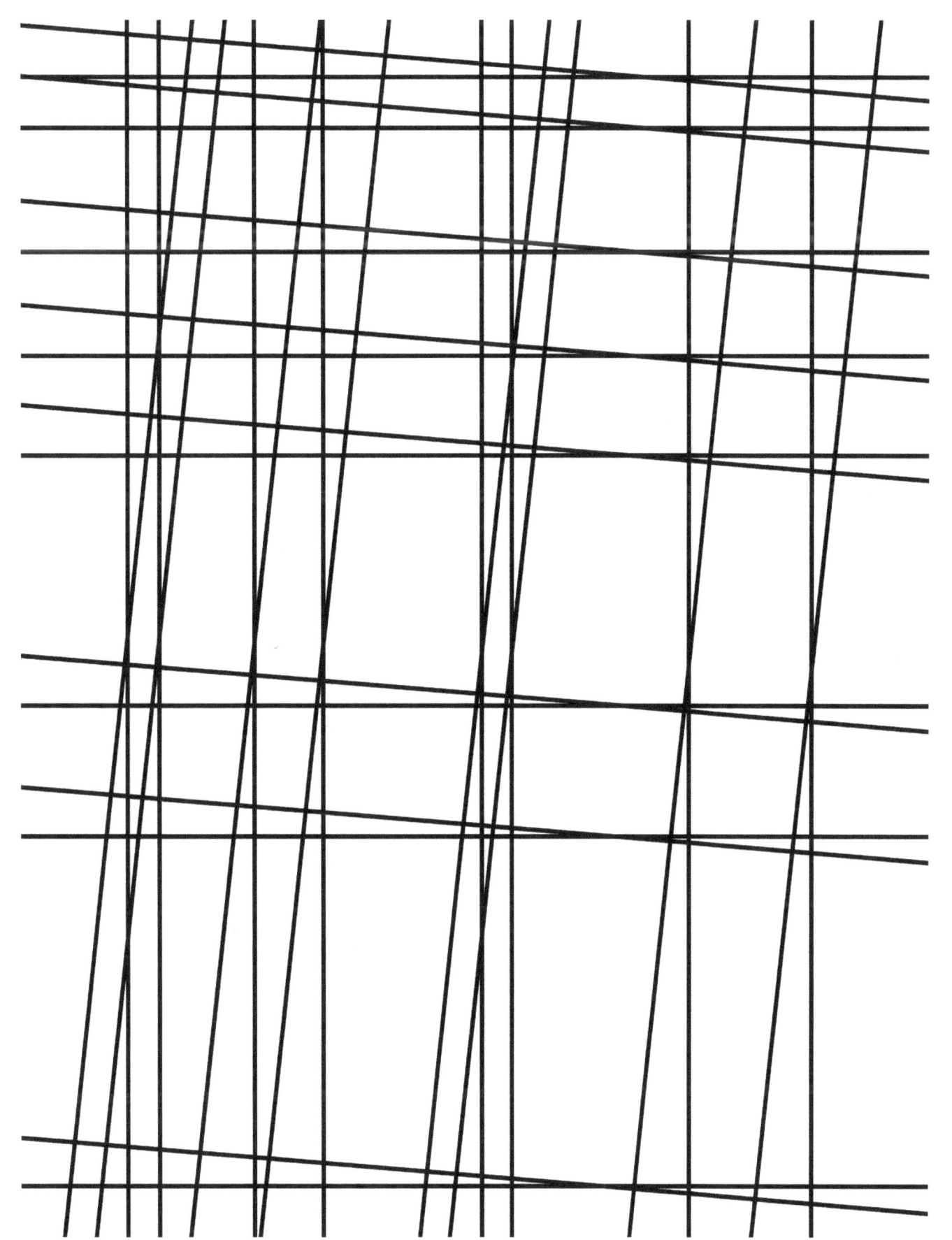

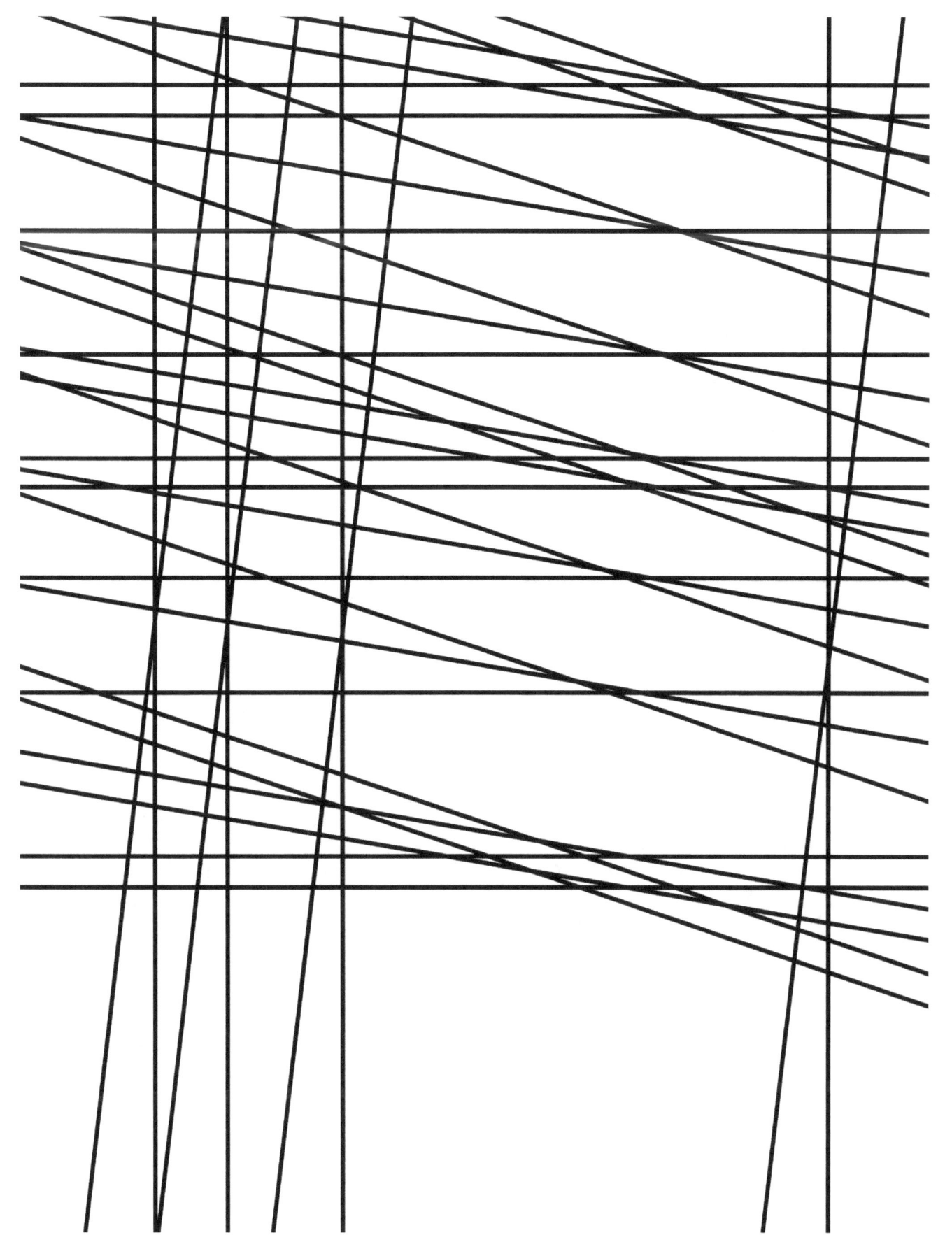

Adele Kuvittaja

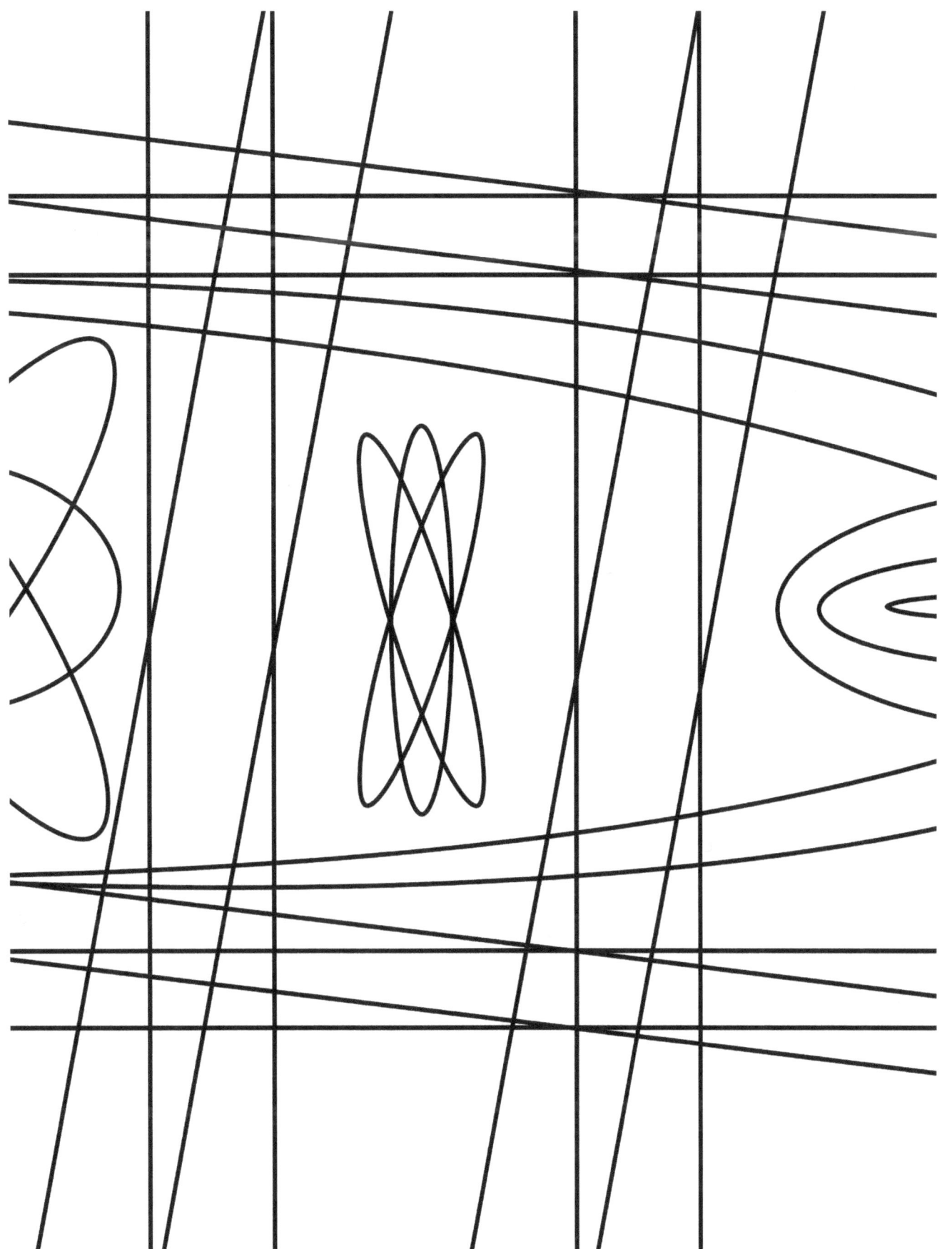

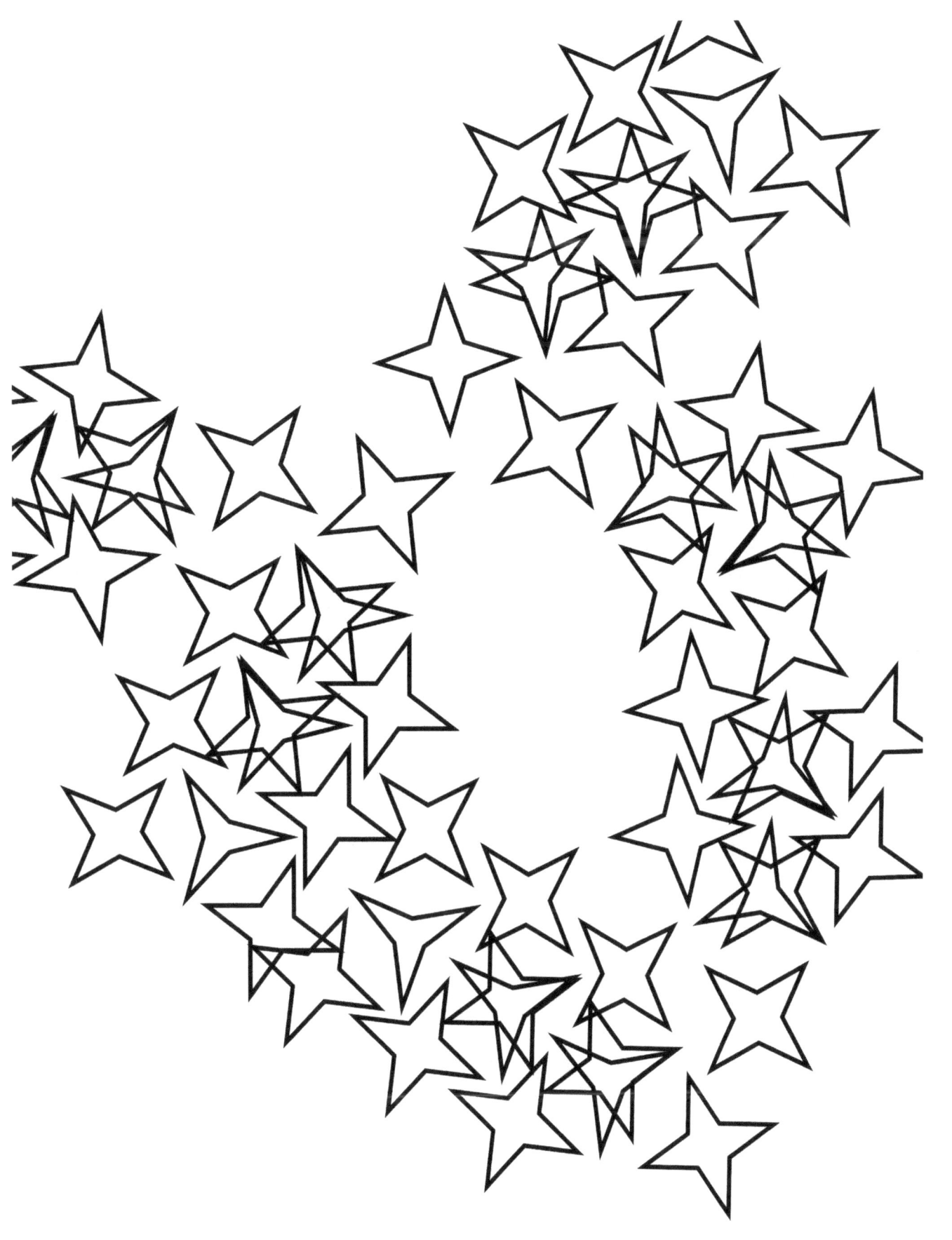

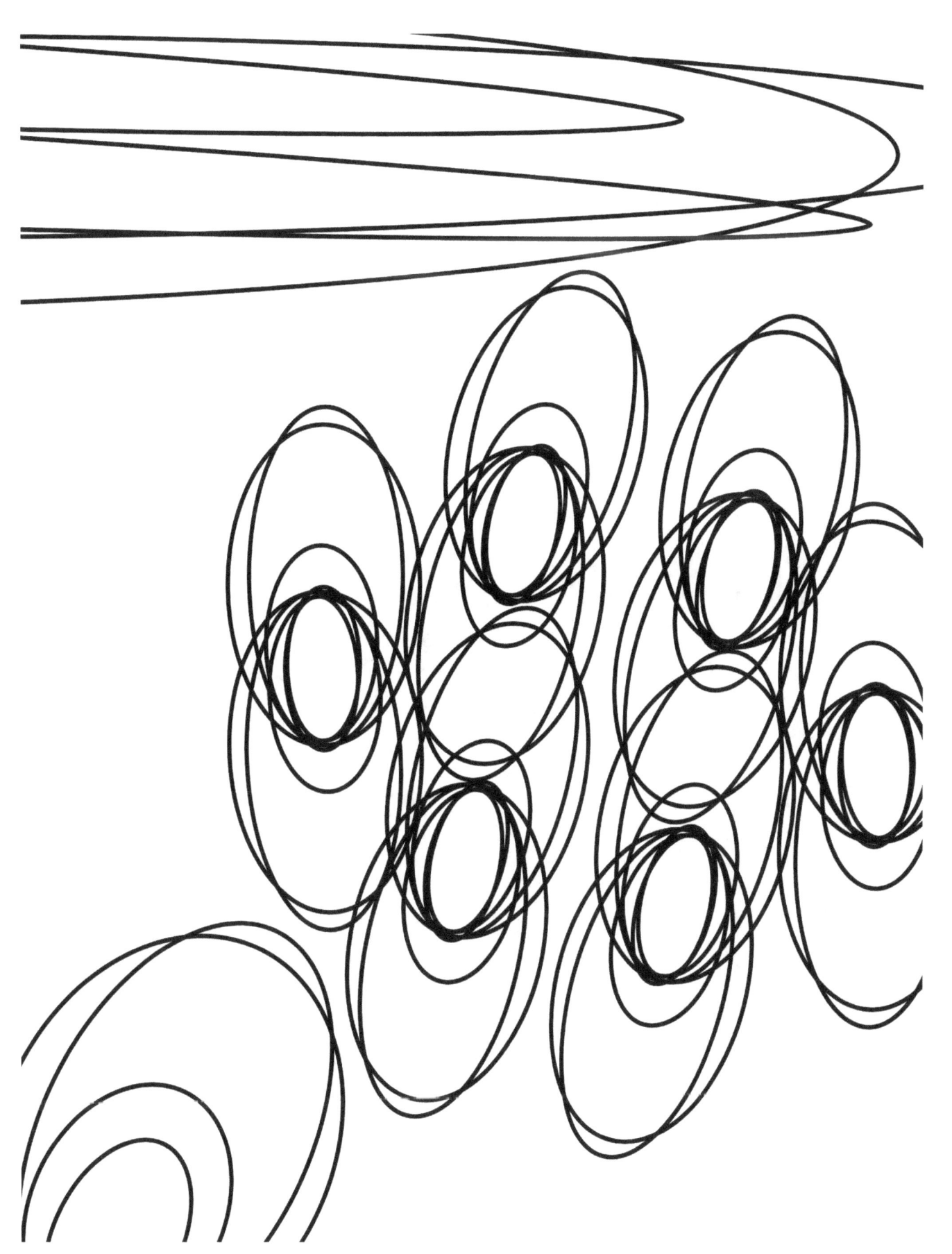

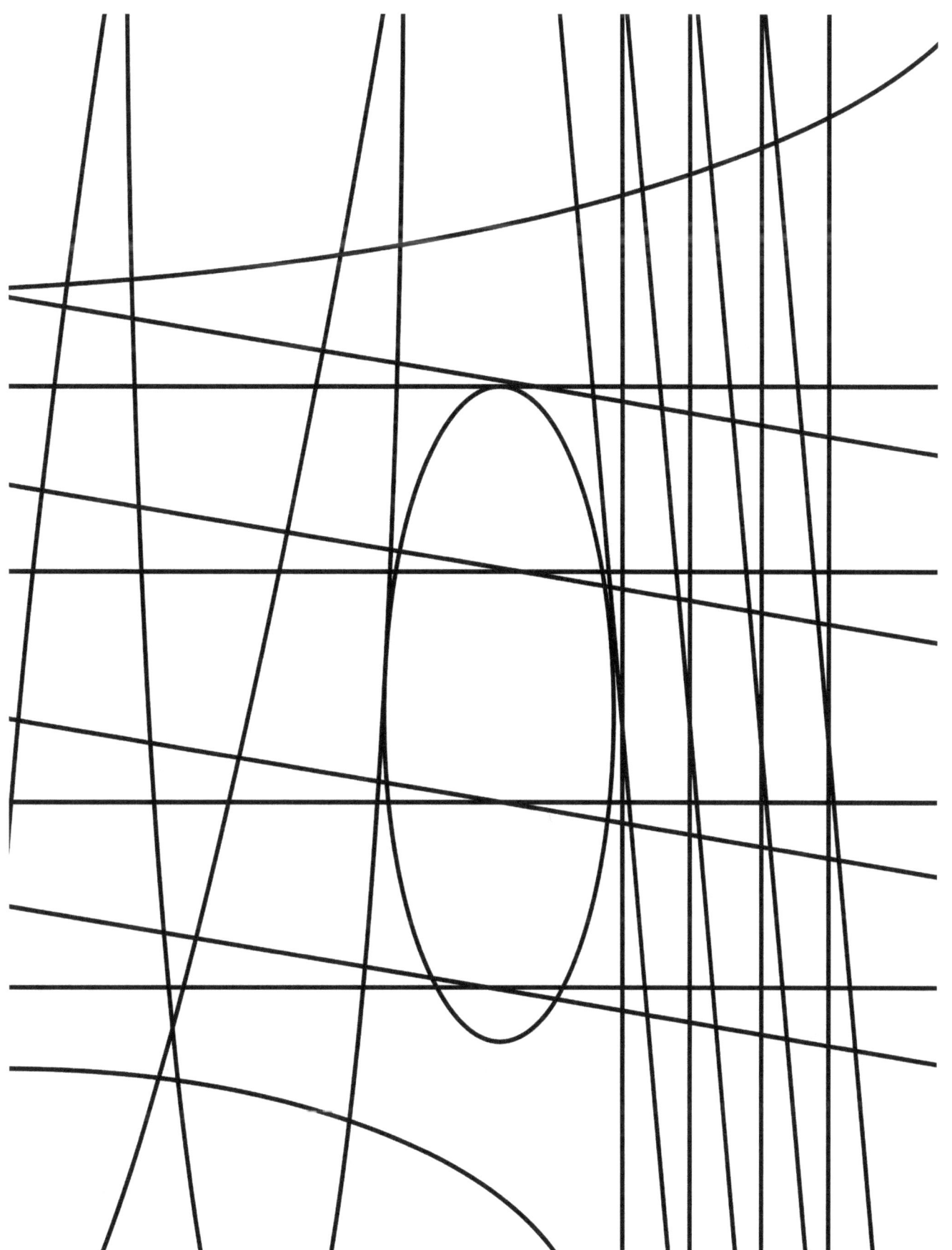

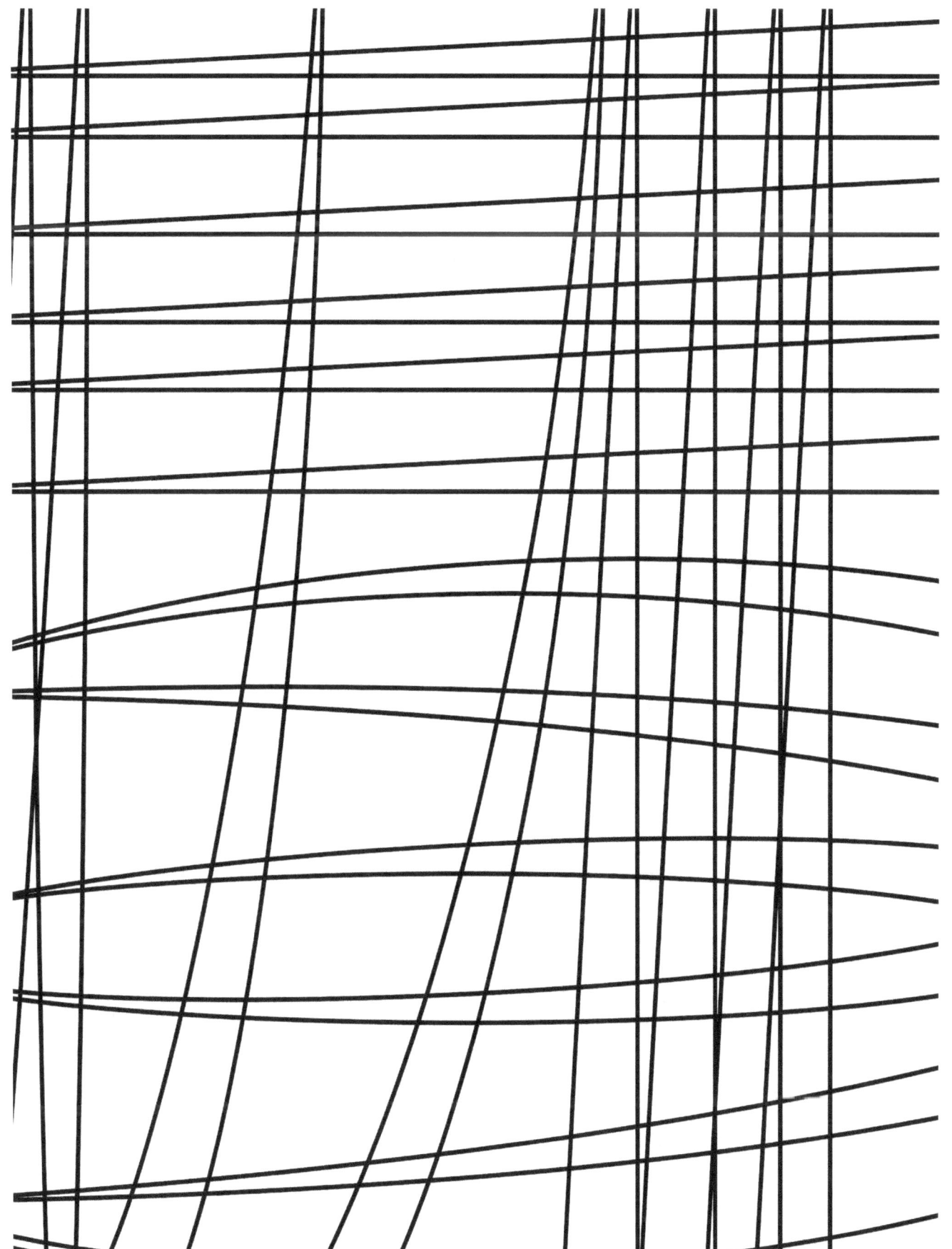

Abstract #25
Adele Kuvittaja

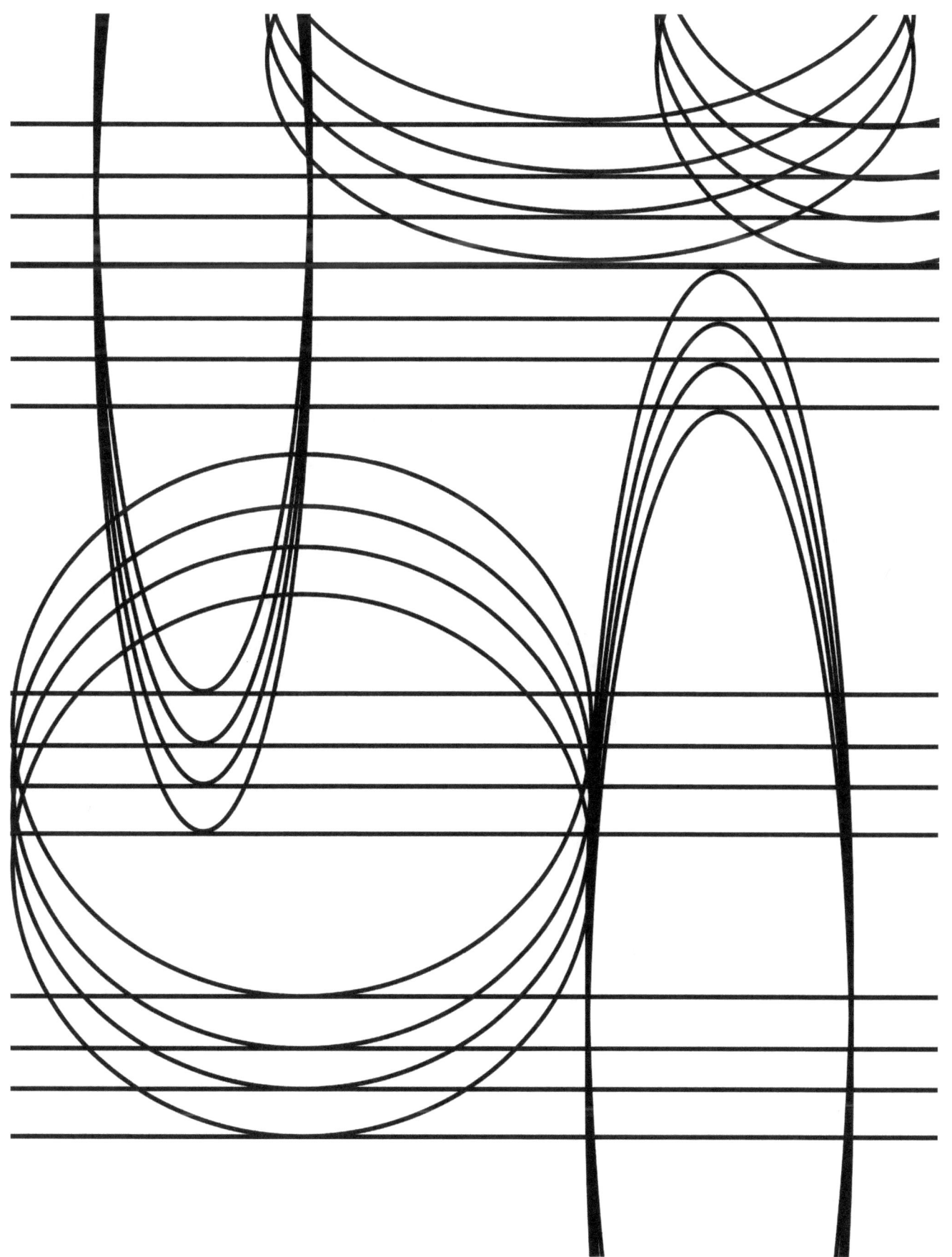

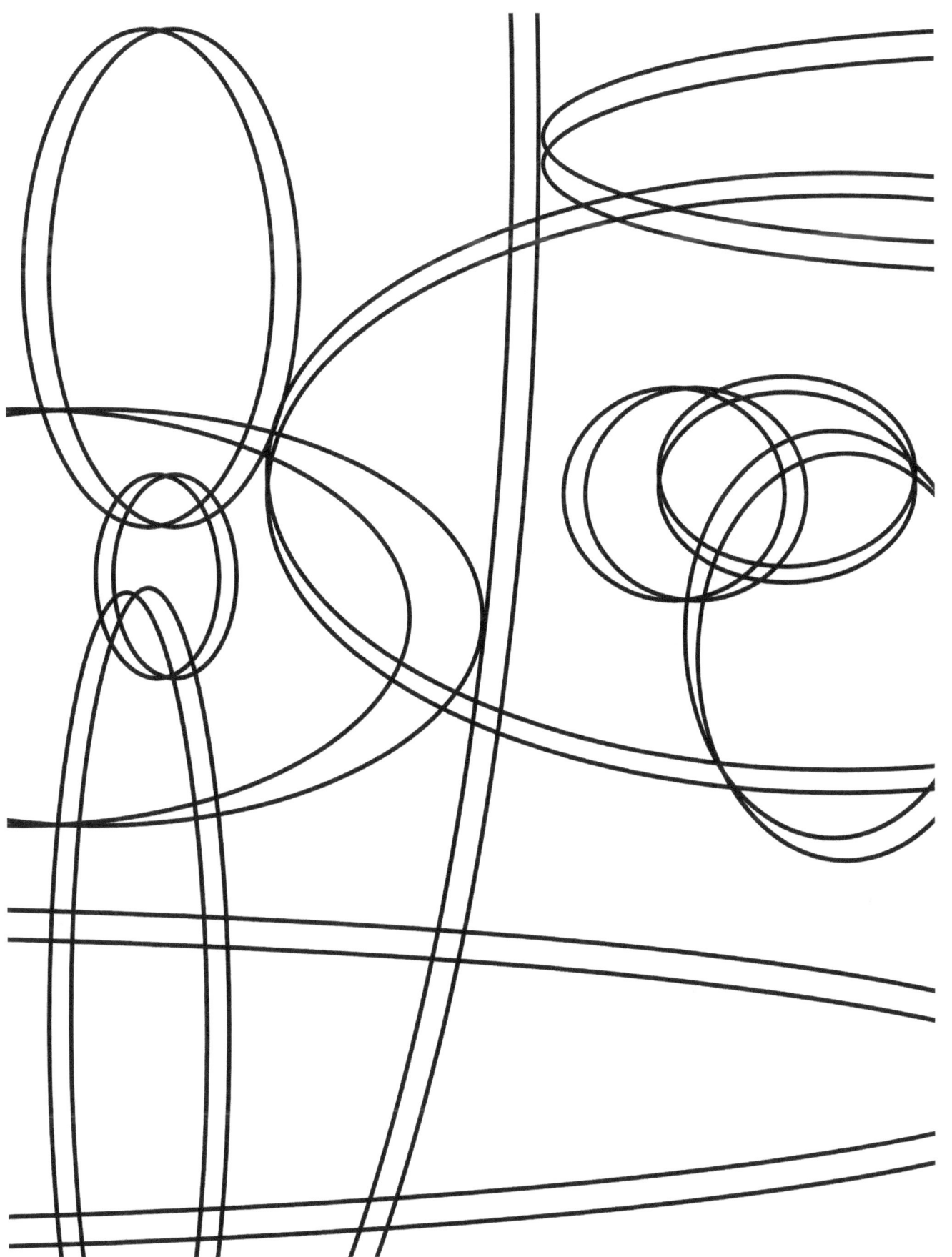

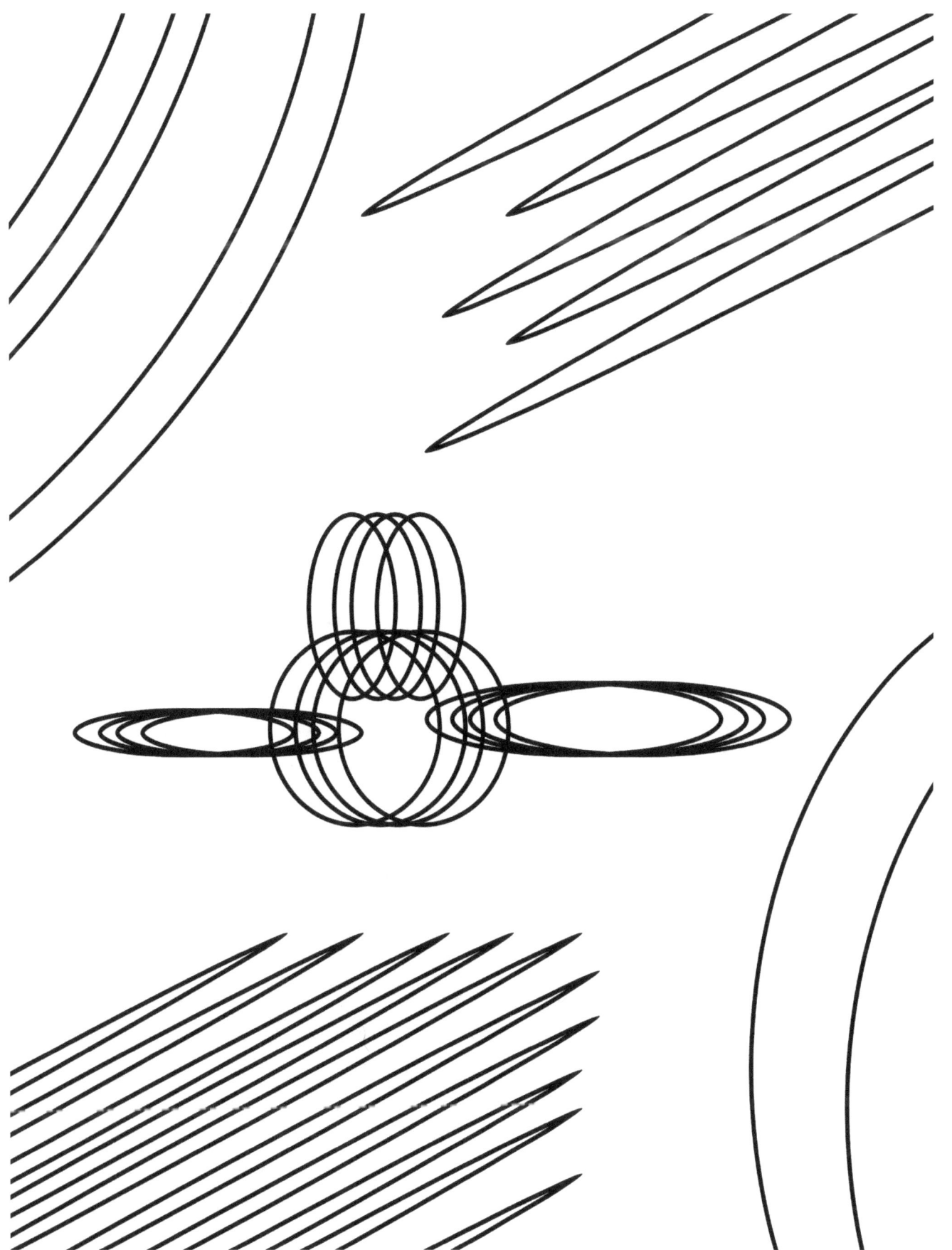

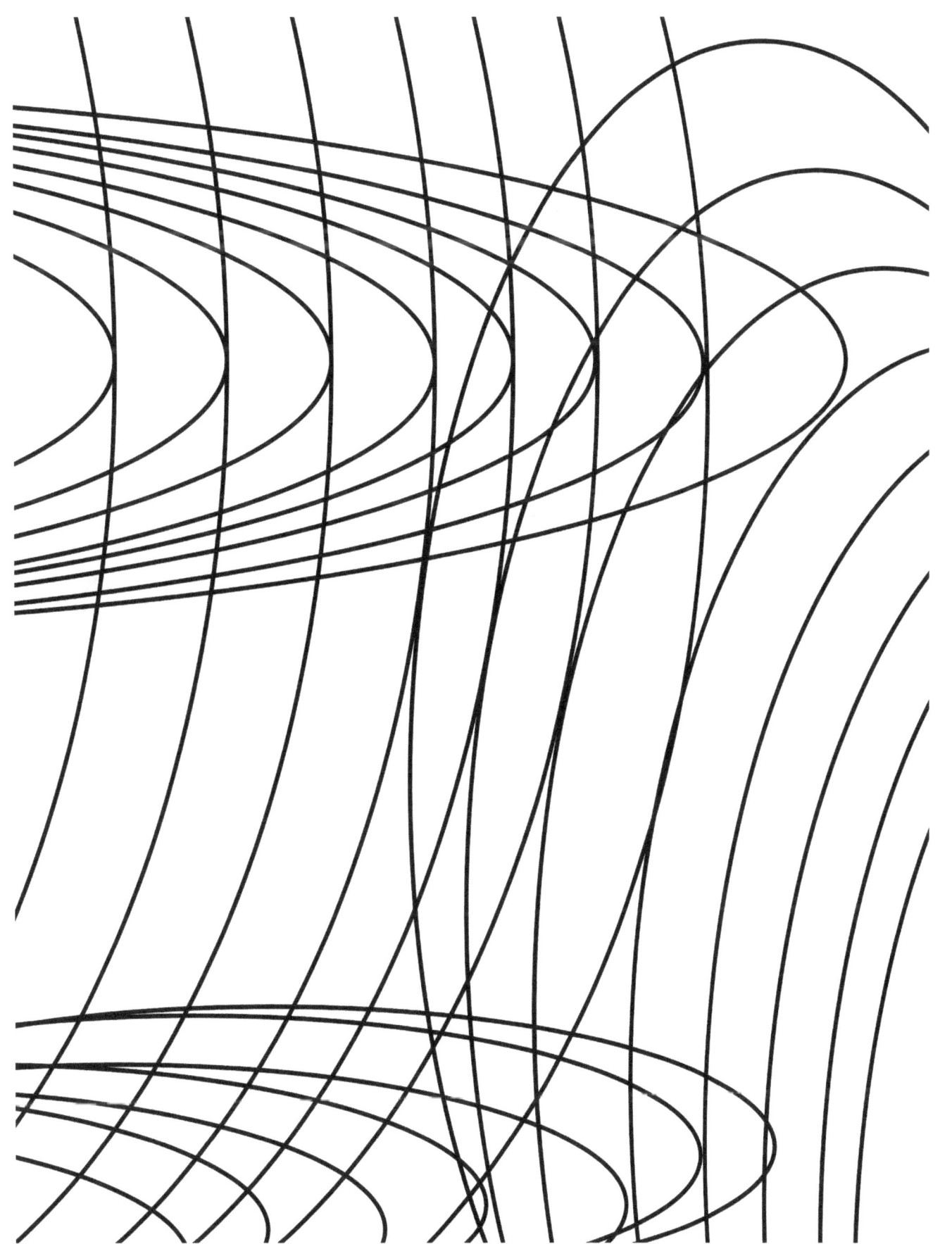

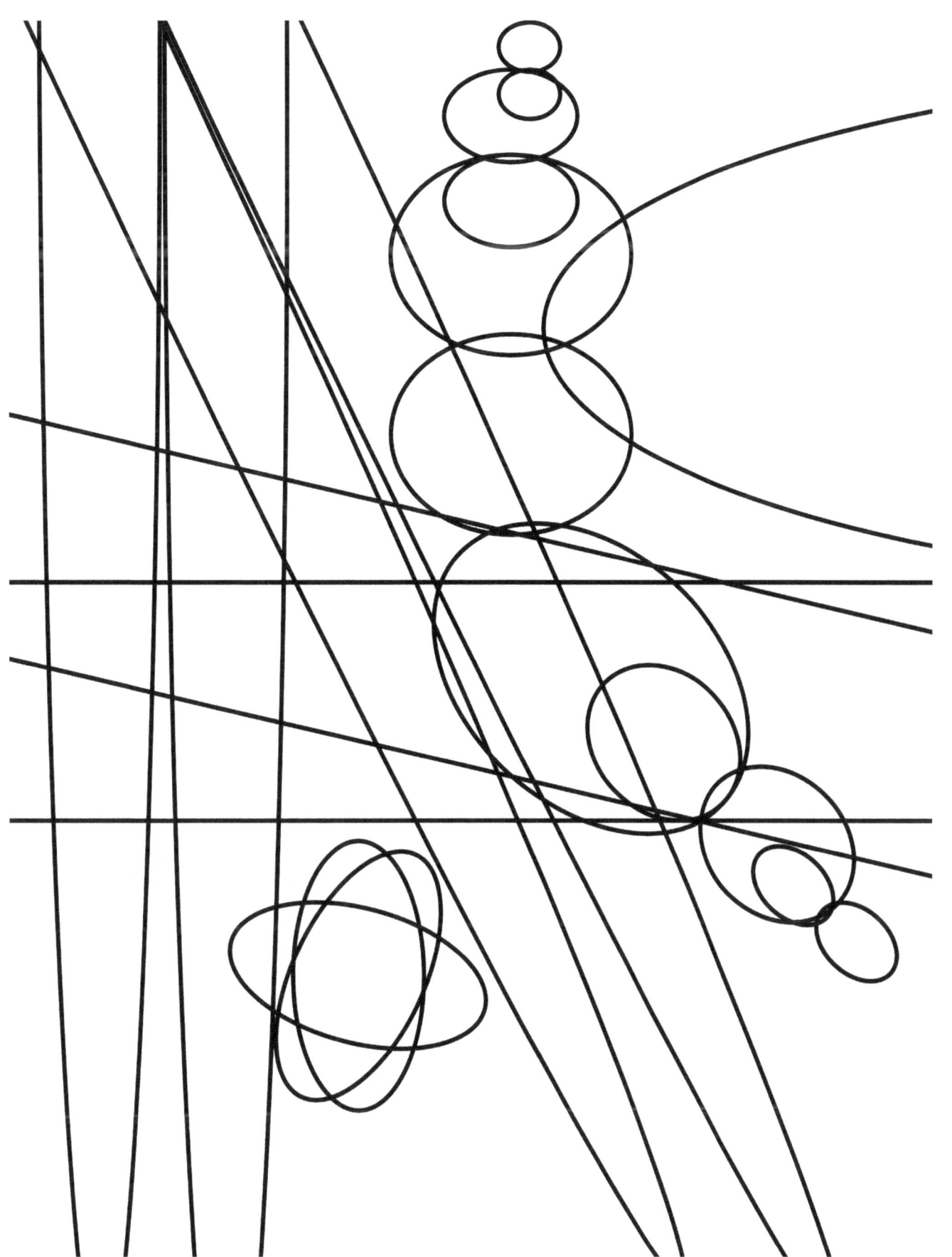

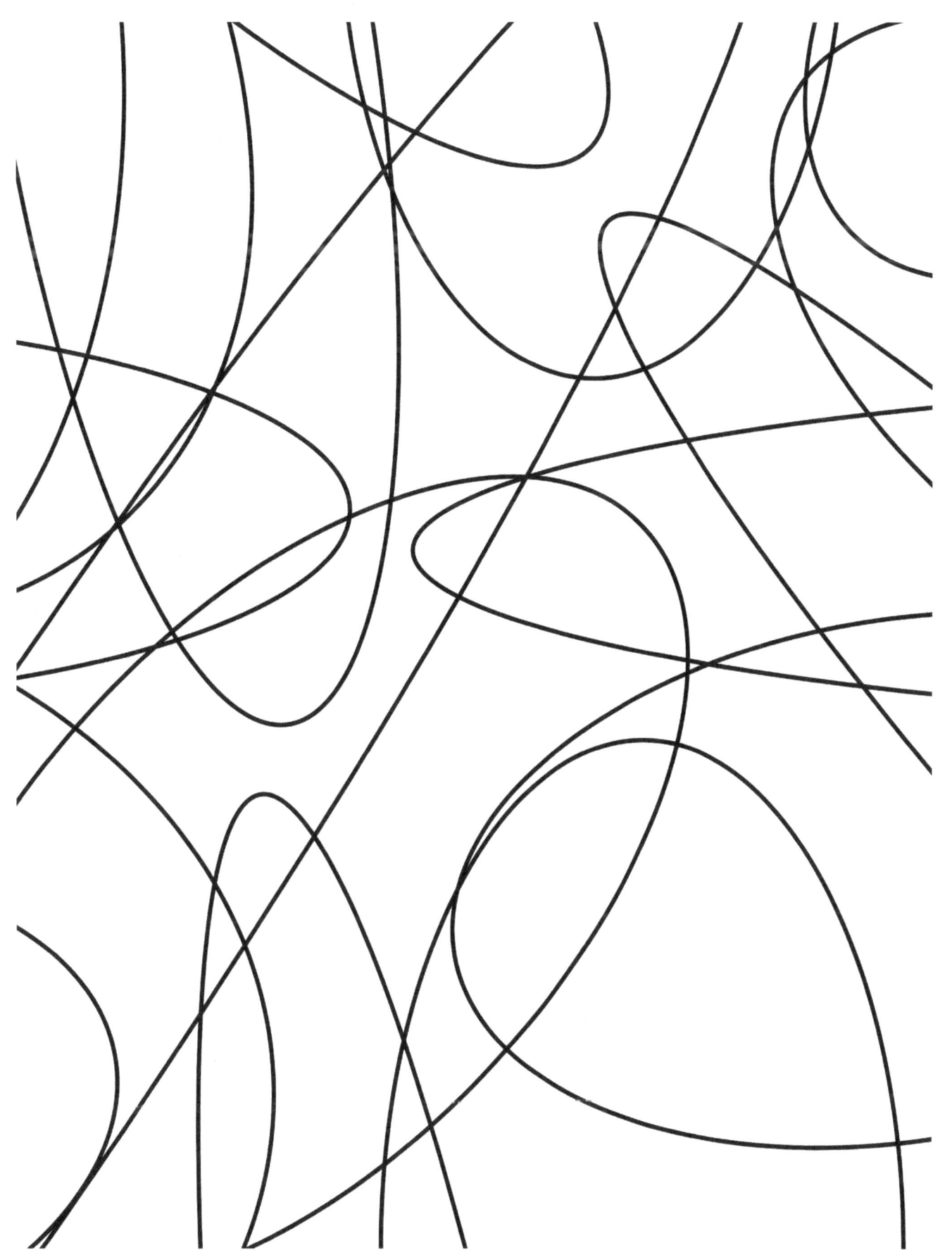

Continue the fun with

B

is for
Bicycle

ADELE KUVITTAJA

www.ingramcontent.com/pod-product-compliance
Lightning Source LLC
Chambersburg PA
CBHW082303200526
45168CB00017B/2765